SRA
Language through Literature

Level 2

Terry Dodds

A Division of The **McGraw-Hill** Companies

Columbus, Ohio

The author wishes to acknowledge the contributions of the team of writers who dedicated many hours of work to this program: Andrew Cameron, Dawn Dodds, Marvin Dodds, Marika Loschiavo and Rick Williams. Special recognition is given to Rick Williams for the unique and creative contributions to the drama and music lessons that he wrote. Thanks are expressed to Jill Cross and Lois Mason for inspiring the author with what they accomplish as teachers of young children. Appreciation is expressed to Ricky Recordo Enterprises © for permission to use their original song and poems in this program.

www.sra4kids.com

SRA/McGraw-Hill

A Division of The **McGraw·Hill** *Companies*

Send all inquiries to:
SRA/McGraw-Hill
8787 Orion Place
Columbus, OH 43240-4027

Printed in the United States of America.

ISBN 0-07-572178-3

3 4 5 6 7 8 9 POH 06 05 04 03

Contents

What Is Language through Literature?

The *Language through Literature* program is a series of direct instruction resource guides that will allow you to help your students make the important connection between basic language skills and literature. Each lesson is based on an easily available, excellent quality children's book. Some are award-winning titles, and all have been chosen because they are of appropriate interest and reading level.

The Guide

This Level 2 guide is designed for you to use in primary classrooms where children are beginning to become more independent readers. Using the guide, you will introduce the children to basic literary structures such as problem-centered linear and circle stories, descriptive stories, fiction and nonfiction, explaining stories, and various forms of poetry. You will present grammar and the correct use of punctuation through short language skill development activities. As children are introduced to editing and proofreading strategies, they will bring written expression from draft to final copy. You will teach dictionary skills using an easy-to-understand, vocabulary–adjusted, dictionary format that is easy for your young students to read and understand. Through the easy-to-follow lesson scripting, you will encourage the children to ask questions as they learn about their world through literature. You will then present them with effective strategies for writing a fairy tale and for completing a report about dinosaurs.

Application

As they complete the lessons, the children will develop a personal framework into which they can add new information and concepts. As this framework grows, the children will develop the ability to see the patterns that are necessary for organizing information and concepts. This organizing of information into patterns makes it possible for children to react to and use new learning in a personal way. For example, as the children look for story patterns and study various literary genres in the books they read, they develop a sense of beginning, middle, and ending. Later they use this plan for writing their own stories and reports.

Your students will be involved in activities and projects that are designed to allow them to interact successfully and enthusiastically with many different genres of children's literature including historical fiction, folktales, legends, myths and fairy tales. The children will have many opportunities to be speakers, listeners, and viewers. As you present the lessons, the children will be challenged to express their ideas individually, in small groups, or to the whole class. You can reinforce the conventions of being good listeners and speakers in every lesson. The lessons will help you introduce your students to a wide variety of media and technology that they can use for gaining information and presenting their ideas to others.

Scheduling

At Level 2 of *Language through Literature,* you will read a new book to the children during each lesson. It is easy to fit the lessons into your classroom schedule. You may choose to teach a whole lesson in one day or break apart the activities and teach them over the course of a week. Following are some possible scheduling options.

Option 1

Teach a lesson over the course of a week. On Monday, teach the Language Skills Development portion of the lesson. On Tuesday, ask the children to make predictions and read the story aloud. On Wednesday, discuss the book. On Thursday, begin the activities. On Friday, complete the activities.

Option 2

Teach a lesson throughout the day. Use the short Language Skills Development portion of the lesson as an opening exercise for the school day, have a story-reading time later in the morning, and complete an art and writing activity during an afternoon art period.

Option 3

Designate one day each week as a literature day and teach an entire lesson. Note: If you choose this option, be aware that some lessons may need more than one day to complete. These lessons may be extended over more than one week.

Option 4

Teach strands from the program in one block. Here are some examples. (1) You might use the Language Skills Development strand as an opening exercise each day. (2) Once the children become familiar with the basic editing and proofreading formats, you can expand upon and use them as a short daily exercise. (3) You can pull the fairy tale or dinosaur lessons from the program and teach them in a block as a mini-unit.

How Do I Present the Lessons?

The lessons in *Language through Literature* provide you with an organized pattern for sharing books with your class and for inviting children's responses to the literature. The engaging and well-illustrated children's books in the program need little introduction, and the children will eagerly become involved with them. Through the lesson activities, they will learn critical thinking skills and how to analyze literature as well as material presented through media other than books. The lessons will also provide you with background information for literary forms, such as historical fiction, legends, folk tales and fairy tales, to help in your presentation of the lessons.

Each lesson varies considerably in the amount of time it will take you to present it. You need to allow sufficient time for student responses, quality writing and artwork, and completion of other activities. The time required for the main part of each literature lesson is dependent upon the length of the book and the amount of time you allow for discussion. As your students become more confident and competent writers, the time for written activities will vary greatly.

In some parts of the lesson, you will ask the children to respond chorally to a hand or voice signal. The choral responses will help the children maintain a higher level of active involvement in the lesson. At other times, you will call on a child or on different children to express their ideas.

Always have the book available for the children to look at during free time. You might want to create a library corner where several copies of the book are available plus additional titles that are similar in topic or are by the same author or illustrator. Invite the children to make comparisons among the books. See each lesson for related titles.

How Can I Use the Writing Process to Improve the Writing of My Students?

Your students will have many opportunities to produce original pieces of writing in this program. The Language Skills Development strand of the program introduces your students to basic language skills that will enable your students to bring their writing from draft to final copy.

The writing process in this program starts with giving your students an opportunity to generate and share a wide variety of ideas before they write. The planning process is facilitated through the use of specially designed planning sheets and writing frames. Writing frames and planning sheets provide your students with organizers that will help them focus on a central idea and write stories that include important story elements such as characters, setting, problem, attempts at solution, and solution. Planning sheets may be used by your students as an evaluation tool to determine if they have achieved the purpose for writing.

As your students revise, edit, and proofread their writing, encourage them to evaluate their own writing and that of others. Have your students work with editing and proofreading partners, so that they learn to help others apply the conventions of standard English and that they learn to comment constructively on the work of others.

Expect your students to spell words taught in formal spelling lessons or that are found on class charts correctly and to apply the grammar, usage, and punctuation strategies taught in the program. Encourage your students to use references such as dictionaries, charts, and word lists to find information and the correct spellings of words.

Lesson 1

Stories and books are fun. We are going to work together to explore and learn about books and literature. You also will learn about writing and making books of your own.

Literature

> # *Dumpling Soup*
>
> ## by Jama Kim Rattigan
>
> ## Illustrated by Lillian Hsu-Flanders

Prereading

Examining the Book

This is the first book that I am going to share with you. The title of this book is *Dumpling Soup.* What's the title of today's book? (Signal.) Dumpling Soup.

The author of this story is Jama (JAY mah) Kim Rattigan. Who is the author of *Dumpling Soup*? (Signal.) *Jama Kim Rattigan.*

The illustrator of this book is Lillian Hsu (soo)-Flanders. Who is the illustrator of *Dumpling Soup*? (Signal.) *Lillian Hsu-Flanders.*

Making Predictions

> **Note:** Many of the activities in this literature program depend on children examining the outside cover of the book. Make an effort to obtain a copy with a dustcover or illustration on the front and back. If this is not possible, use the illustration on the title page of the picture book, if there is one. The first illustration in the story may also be used for making predictions.

When we tell what we think the story is about we are making a **prediction.** What are we doing when we tell what we think the story is about? (Signal.) *Making a prediction.*

(Assign each child a partner. Show children the front and back covers of the book.) Look at the front and back covers. Tell your partner what you think the story will be about. (Allow about one minute for sharing predictions.)

Raise your hand if you would like to tell us your prediction of what you think the story will be about. (Call on three different children. Accept reasonable responses.)

Using a Glossary

(Show children the glossary at the beginning of the book.) This is a glossary. A **glossary** is a very short dictionary. What is a glossary? (Signal.) *A very short dictionary.* This story uses words from many different languages. The glossary tells us what these words mean. Why does this book have a glossary? (Call on a child. Idea: *To tell us what the words from different languages mean.*)

The languages used in this book are English, Hawaiian, Japanese, and Korean. What languages are used in this book? (Signal.) *English, Hawaiian, Japanese, and Korean.* (Print the word **litchi** on the chalkboard.) This word says **litchi.** What word? (Signal.) *Litchi.* (Print the two ways to pronounce **litchi** on the chalkboard.) The glossary tells us that there are two ways to pronounce **litchi.** (Point to **lie-chee.**) The first way is lie-chee. What's the first way to pronounce **litchi**? (Signal.) *Lie-chee.* The Hawaiian way to pronounce **litchi** is **Lee-chee.** What's the Hawaiian pronunciation? (Signal.) *Lee-chee.*

(Print **tree with a nutlike fruit** on the chalkboard.) The glossary tells us what the word means. (Point to the meaning.) **Litchi** means a tree with a nutlike fruit. What does **litchi** mean? (Signal.) *Tree with a nutlike fruit.* (Repeat process for one Hawaiian word, one Japanese word, and one Korean word.)

Listen carefully while I read the story. When you hear a word from another language, raise your hand and we will look up its meaning in the glossary. (As you read the story, emphasize words from another language to help the children know when to ask for a word. Have children say the word and its meaning.)

Reading the Story

I'm going to read the story aloud to you and show you the pictures. After I read the story to you, we will talk about the story. (Read the story with minimal interruptions; this ensures that the children hear the story in its entirety, thus helping them develop a better sense of story. Occasionally you may find it beneficial to discuss parts of the story that are complicated or have unfamiliar vocabulary. Encourage children to check the illustrations, the structures of words, and context to help them decipher unknown words and their meanings.)

Discussing the Book

Story Pattern

Most books have a pattern. Let's see if we can figure out the pattern for this book. You tell me what happened in the story and I'll write it on the chalkboard.

> **Note:** As children retell the story, make a story map of the main story events on the chalkboard, similar to the following sample.

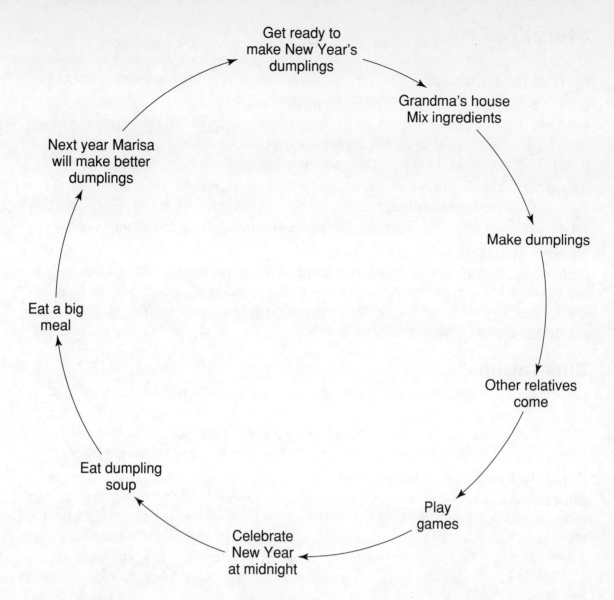

Get ready to make New Year's dumplings

Grandma's house Mix ingredients

Make dumplings

Other relatives come

Play games

Celebrate New Year at midnight

Eat dumpling soup

Eat a big meal

Next year Marisa will make better dumplings

(Discuss the sequence of story events briefly to construct the story map.)

(Point to the story map that is on the chalkboard.) Look at the shape of this story. It's a circle. This story starts and ends with Marisa getting ready to celebrate New Year's Eve. The pattern for this story is a circle. What's the pattern for this story? (Signal.) *A circle.*

Characters and Setting

All stories have a beginning, a middle, and an ending. The word **character** tells who is in the story. What does the word **character** tell? (Signal.) *Who is in the story.* The beginning of a story tells about the characters that are in the story. What does the beginning of a story tell about? (Signal.) *The characters that are in the story.* Who are the important characters in *Dumpling Soup*? (Call on different children. Idea: *Marisa, Grandma, various family members.*)

The beginning also tells about the setting of the story. The **setting** tells where and when the story happens. What does the setting tell? (Signal.) *Where and when the story happens.* Where does this story happen? (Call on a child. Ideas: *Oahu, Hawaii, at Grandma's house.*) When does this story happen? (Call on a child. Idea: *Around New Year's Eve.*)

Story Problem

The beginning of a story often has a problem that changes the everyday life of at least one of the characters. What problem did Marisa have in the story? (**Call on a child.** Idea: *She was worried that her dumplings weren't good.*)

In stories with a problem, the problem changes the feelings of the characters, so they decide to do something about the problem. How did Marisa feel about her problem? (**Call on a child.** Ideas: *Worried, upset, embarrassed.*)

The middle of a story tells what the character does to try to solve a problem. This is called the **attempt at solution.** What did Marisa decide to do about her problem? (**Call on a child.** Idea: *She tried very hard to make her dumplings as good as those of her aunties.*)

The end of the story tells what happened that finally solved the problem. This is called the **solution** to the problem. What was the solution to Marisa's problem? (**Call on a child.** Ideas: *Uncle Myung Ho, Grandma, everyone likes Marisa's dumplings. The dumplings tasted better than they looked.*)

Illustrations

Let's look at the illustrations that Lillian Hsu-Flanders made. There are many different ways to make illustrations for a book: you can paint them; you can draw them with a pen or pencil; you can make them with markers, crayons, or chalk. How do you think Lillian Hsu-Flanders made her illustrations? (**Call on a child.** Idea: *With watercolors.*)

(**Show children the last illustration in the book.**) This kind of picture is called a family portrait. What is this kind of picture called? (**Signal.**) *A family portrait.* This family portrait is a watercolor painting. What else could you use to show a family portrait? (**Call on a child.** Idea: *A camera to take a photograph.*) The illustrator shows this family portrait glued into a special kind of book. Raise your hand if you can tell us what we call a book into which photographs are glued. (**Call on a child.** Ideas: *A scrapbook, a photo album.*)

Recalling Information

Let's remember some of the things we learned about *Dumpling Soup,* and I'll write them down for you.

Note: Create a cumulative wall chart for recording information from the "Recalling Information" activity in this literature lesson. Draw it on large sheets of chart paper because you will be adding to it during various lessons throughout the program. See following sample.

Recalling Information

Title	Important Characters	Beginning			Middle	Ending
		Setting (Where, When)	Problem	Feeling	Attempts to Solve the Problem	Solution to the Problem

What is the title of today's book? (Signal.) *Dumpling Soup.* (Write the title on the chart.)

Who are the important characters in this story? (Call on different children. Ideas: *Marisa, Grandma, various family members.* Write characters on chart.)

Tell me a word that describes each character. (Call on different children. Accept two words for each character. Record on chart.)

The setting of a story tells where and when the story happened. What does the setting of a story tell? (Signal.) *Where and when the story happened.* Where does this story take place? (Call on a child. Ideas: *Oahu, Hawaii, at Grandma's house.* Record on chart.)

When does this story take place? (Call on a child. Idea: *Around New Year's Eve.* Record on chart.)

What was Marisa's problem in the story? (Call on a child. Idea: *She was worried that her dumplings weren't good.* Record on chart.)

How did that problem make Marisa feel? (Call on a child. Ideas: *Worried, upset, embarrassed.* Record on chart.)

How did Marisa attempt to solve her problem? (Call on a child. Idea: *She tried very hard to make her dumplings as good as those of her aunties.* Record on chart.)

What was the solution to Marisa's problem? (Call on a child. Ideas: *Uncle Myung Ho, Grandma, everyone likes Marisa's dumplings. The dumplings tasted better than they looked.* Record on chart.)

Activity

Writing Informational Text/Writing Three Steps in Sequence/Expository Writing

Title: *Making Dumplings*
   Time Required: 30 minutes
   Materials Required: BLM 1, one copy for each child

Procedure

1. (Give each child a copy of BLM 1.) Today you are going to write the instructions for making dumplings. When we write **instructions,** we write the steps for doing an activity. What do we do when we write instructions? (Signal.) *We write the steps for doing an activity.*

2. (Show children the second and third pages of the story. Read page 3 aloud.) Everyone is making dumplings in this part of the story.

3. Touch item 1 on your sheet. My turn to read item 1. Go shopping to buy ingredients. Buy blank. Your turn. Read item 1. (Signal.) *Go shopping to buy ingredients. Buy blank.* **Ingredients** are what you put in a recipe when you cook. What are ingredients? (Signal.) *What you put in a recipe when you cook.* What ingredients did Marisa's mother buy? (Call on a child. Ideas: *Piles of beef, pork, vegetables; and dumpling wrappers.* Repeat process for each step of the directions. How to wrap dumplings is on page 5 of the story. How to cook dumplings is on page 6 of the story.)

Technology

(You may make the blank writing frame available on the computer using a word processing program or children's writing program. The children may then insert their parts of the frame. Have children highlight and select different fonts for their writing.)

ADDITIONAL LITERATURE

Following are some additional titles that your students may enjoy during and following this lesson.

Stone Soup by Heather Forest

Mei Mei Loves the Morning by Margaret Holloway Tsubakiyama

Flyaway Girl by Ann Grifalconi

Making Dumpling Soup

1. Go shopping to buy ingredients. Buy _____
   _____.

2. Chop ingredients.

3. Mix ingredients in a big metal pan. These are some of the
   ingredients: _____
   _____.

   Leave overnight in the refrigerator.

4. Place a dumpling wrapper on the table.

5. Put filling in _____.

6. Dip fingers in _____.

7. Fold _____.

8. Pinch _____.

9. Cook dumplings in a big pot full of _____.

Lesson 2

Language Skill Development

Alphabetical Order/Dictionary Skills

Title: *Using a Dictionary*
   Time Required: 15 minutes
   Materials Required: BLM 2A, 2B, 2C, 2D, 2E, 2F, one copy for each child

Note: You will need to make enough photocopies of BLM 2A through 2F to make a dictionary for each child. Staple the left margin three times to make a book.

Note: Refer to a poster or banner of the alphabet displayed prominently in the classroom for the alphabet review. Children may also review by singing the *Alphabet Song.*

Today you will learn how to use a dictionary. What will you learn how to use today? (Signal.) *A dictionary.* Words in a dictionary are listed in alphabetical order. How are the words in a dictionary listed? (Signal.) *In alphabetical order.* Words listed in alphabetical order follow the order of the letters in the alphabet. What order do words listed alphabetically follow? (Signal.) *The letters in the alphabet.* Let's review the letters of the alphabet together. You say the letters with me. (Signal.) (Point to each letter on the poster as you say it.) *A, b, c, . . . x, y, z.*

(Touch the letters as you say them.) The letters **a, b, c, d, e, f,** and **g** are the first part of the alphabet. What letters are the first part of the alphabet? (Signal.) *A, b, c, d, e, f, and g.* (Touch the letters as you say them.) The letters **h, i, j, k, l, m, n, o, p, q, r, s,** and **t** are the middle part of the alphabet. What letters are the middle part of the alphabet? (Signal.) *H, i, j, k, l, m, n, o, p, q, r, s, and t.* (Touch the letters as you say them.) The letters **u, v, w, x, y,** and **z** are the last part of the alphabet. What letters are the last part of the alphabet? (Signal.) *U, v, w, x, y, and z.* (Repeat until firm.)

(Pass out a copy of the dictionary to each child.) Everybody, touch the words at the top of page 1 in your dictionary. (Check.) This says **Parts of the Dictionary.** What does this say? (Signal.) *Parts of the dictionary.* Today you will learn what the different parts of the dictionary are called. What will you learn today? (Signal.) *What the different parts of the dictionary are called.*

Touch item number 1 in the dictionary example. (Check.) This says **entry word.** What does this say? (Signal.) *Entry word.* The entry word is written with bold, dark letters. How is the entry word written? (Signal.) *With bold, dark letters.* The entry word shows how to spell the word. What does the entry word show? (Signal.) *How to spell the word.*

The entry word for this example is **baby.** What is the entry word for this example? (Signal.) *Baby.* Raise your hand if you can tell us how to spell **baby** by looking at the bold entry word. (Call on a child.) *B-a-b-y.* (Write the word on the chalkboard.)

Touch item number 2 in the dictionary example. (Check.) This says **part of speech.** What does this say? (Signal.) *Part of speech.* The part of speech tells you what kind of word it is. What does the part of speech tell you? (Signal.) *What kind of word it is.* You will learn more about parts of speech later this year.

Touch item number 3 in the dictionary example. (Check.) This says **definition.** What does this say? (Signal.) *Definition.* The definition tells you what the word means. What does the definition tell you? (Signal.) *What the word means.*

Let's read together the definition for the entry word **baby.** (Signal.) *A very young child; infant.* What is a **baby**? (Signal.) *A very young child; infant.*

Touch item number 4 in the dictionary example. (Check.) This says **sentence example.** What does this say? (Signal.) *Sentence example.* The sentence example shows you how to use the entry word in a sentence. What does the sentence example show you? (Signal.) *How to use the entry word in a sentence.* The sentence example is written in italics. How is the sentence example written? (Signal.) *In italics.* Let's read the sentence example for the entry word **baby** together. (Signal.) *The baby is learning how to walk.*

Listen. Sometimes a word means more than one thing. Can a word sometimes mean more than one thing? (Signal.) *Yes.* Touch item number 5 in the dictionary example. (Check.) This is a bold number 1. What is this? (Signal.) *A bold number one.* This bold number 1 tells you the first thing the entry word means. What does the bold number 1 tell you? (Signal.) *The first thing that the entry word means.* Raise your hand if you can remember the first definition of the word **baby.** (Call on a child. Idea: *A very young child; infant.*)

Touch item number 6 in the dictionary example. (Check.) This is a bold number 2. What is this? (Signal.) *A bold number 2.* This bold number 2 tells you the second thing the entry word means. What does the bold number 2 tell you? (Signal.) *The second thing that the entry word means.* Let's read the second definition for the entry word **baby** together. (Signal.) *The youngest person in a family or group.* What is the second thing that **baby** means? (Signal.) *The youngest person in a family or group.*

Touch the sentence example for the second definition of the word **baby** in italics. (Check.) Let's read the second sentence example for the entry word **baby** together. (Signal.) *I am the baby of the family.*

Technology

(Children may use children's dictionary software for practice using another format of dictionary.)

Literature

A Chair for My Mother

by Vera B. Williams

Prereading

Examining the Book

This is the next book that I am going to share with you. The title of this book is *A Chair for My Mother*. What's the title of today's book? (Signal.) A Chair for My Mother.

Sometimes the same person writes the story and makes the pictures. Sometimes the author and illustrator are two different people. Vera B. Williams wrote this story and she made the pictures. Did the same person write the story and make the pictures for *A Chair for My Mother*? (Signal.) *Yes.* Vera B. Williams is both the author and the illustrator of this book. Who is the author of *A Chair for My Mother*? (Signal.) *Vera B. Wiliams.* Who is the illustrator of *A Chair for My Mother*? (Signal.) *Vera B. Williams.*

Making Predictions

> **Note:** Many of the activities in this literature program depend on children examining the outside cover of the book. Make an effort to obtain a copy with a dustcover or illustration on the front and back. If this is not possible, use the illustration on the title page of the book, if there is one. The first illustration in the story may also be used for making predictions.

When we tell what we think the story is about we are making a prediction. What are we doing when we tell what we think the story is about? (Signal.) *Making a prediction.*

(Assign each child a partner. Show children the front and back covers of the book.) Look at the front and back covers. Tell your partner what you think the story will be about. (Allow about one minute for sharing predictions.)

Raise your hand if you would like to tell us your prediction of what you think the story will be about. (Call on three different children. Accept reasonable responses.)

Reading the Story

I'm going to read the story aloud to you and show you the pictures. After I read the story to you, we will talk about the story. (Read the story with minimal interruptions. This ensures that the children hear the story in its entirety, thus helping them develop a better sense of story. Occasionally you may find it beneficial to discuss parts of the story that are complicated or have unfamiliar vocabulary. Encourage children to check the illustrations, the structures of words, and context to help them decipher unknown words and their meanings.)

Discussing the Book

Story Pattern

Most books have a pattern. Let's see if we can figure out the pattern for this book. You tell me what happened in the story and I'll write it on the chalkboard.

> **Note:** As children retell the story, make a story map of the main story events on the chalkboard, similar to the following sample.

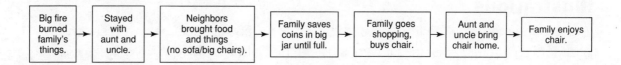

| Big fire burned family's things. | → | Stayed with aunt and uncle. | → | Neighbors brought food and things (no sofa/big chairs). | → | Family saves coins in big jar until full. | → | Family goes shopping, buys chair. | → | Aunt and uncle bring chair home. | → | Family enjoys chair. |

(Discuss the sequence of story events briefly to construct the story map.)

(Point to the story map that is on the chalkboard.) Look at the shape of this story. It's a line. This story starts and ends in different places, so it is called a **linear story.** What do we call a story that starts and ends in different places? (Signal.) *A linear story.*

Characters and Setting

All stories have a beginning, a middle, and an ending. The word **character** tells who is in the story. What does the word **character** tell? (Signal.) *Who is in the story.* The beginning of a story tells about the characters that are in the story. What does the beginning of a story tell about? (Signal.) *The characters that are in the story.* Who are the important characters in *A Chair for My Mother*? (Call on different children. Idea: *The girl, Mama, Grandma.*)

The beginning also tells about the setting of the story. The setting tells where and when the story happens. What does the setting tell? (Signal.) *Where and when the story happens.* Where does this story happen? (Call on a child. Ideas: *The Blue Tile Diner, home, furniture store, city.*)

(Show the children the page with red and yellow tulips.) What do you see in this picture that tells about when this part of the story takes place? (Call on different children. Ideas: *Sunshine, red and yellow tulips.*) Tulips are flowers that bloom only in the spring, so we know that this part of the story takes place during the spring. When does this part of the story take place? (Signal.) *In the spring.*

(Show children the page with the full jar of coins.) Raise your hand if you can remember how much time it took to fill the jar. (Call on a child. Idea: *One year.*)

Story Problem

The beginning of a story often has a problem that changes the everyday life of at least one of the characters. What problem did the girl, Mama, and Grandma have in the story? (Call on a child. Ideas: *Their old house had burned down in a fire. They didn't have a sofa or a big chair.*)

In stories with a problem, the problem changes the feelings of the characters, so they decide to do something about the problem. How did the girl feel about her problem? (Call on a child. Ideas: *Worried about her mother, upset.*)

The middle of a story tells what the character does to try to solve a problem. This is called the attempt at solution. What did the girl and her mother decide to do about their problem? (Call on a child. Idea: *They worked at the diner, saved all their coins in a big jar, and put the money saved from bargains in the jar.*)

The end of the story tells what happened that finally solved the problem. This is called the solution to the problem. What was the solution to the family's problem? (Call on a child. Idea: *The family worked hard and filled the jar together, then wrapped the coins and took them to the bank, and shopped for a new chair.*)

Illustrations

(Point to the medal on the front cover.) This book is special because it won second prize for its pictures. This prize it won is called the Caldecott Medal. What prize did the book *A Chair for My Mother* win? (Signal.) *The Caldecott Medal.*

Let's look at the illustrations that Vera B. Williams made. (Point to the border around the first pair of pages in the story.) A **border** is a picture that goes all around the edge of the page. What is a picture that goes all around the edge of the page called? (Signal.) *A border.* A border often goes together with the story and illustration on that page. The border on this page is made up of little blue tiles. Raise your hand if you can read the name of the diner. (Call on a child.) *Blue Tile Diner.* The blue tiles on the border go with the name of the diner. (Point to the border around the page with the fire engines.) What is the border on this page a picture of? (Signal.) *Fire.* Raise your hand if you can tell us what's happening in this picture. (Call on a child. Idea: *Fire engines are trying to put out the house fire.*)

(Show children the pair of pages where the house is burned to ashes.) Raise your hand if you can tell us what happened in this picture. (Call on a child. Idea: *The house burned down.*) Are there lots of bright colors on these pages? (Signal.) *No.* How does this picture make you feel? (Call on different children. Ideas: *Sad, depressed.*)

(Show children the next pair of pages.) Raise your hand if you can tell us what's happening in this picture. (Call on a child. Idea: *Everyone is bringing things to help the family set up a new house.*) Are there lots of bright colors on these pages? (Signal.) *Yes.* How does this picture make you feel? (Call on different children. Ideas: *Happy, hopeful, cheerful.*)

(Show children the last illustration in the book.) This kind of picture is called a family portrait. What is this kind of picture called? (Signal.) *A family portrait.* This family portrait is a watercolor painting. What else could you use to show a family portrait? (Call on a child. Idea: *A camera to take a photograph.*) The illustrator shows this family portrait glued into a special kind of book. Raise your hand if you can tell us what we call a book into which photographs are glued. (Call on a child. Ideas: *A scrapbook, a photo album.*)

(Show children the page where the mother is sleeping in the kitchen. Circulate among children and point to the radio on top of the refrigerator.) We listen to the radio to learn information and to hear music. Why do we listen to the radio? (Signal.) *To learn information and to hear music.* Raise your hand if you can tell us a kind of information we hear on the radio. (Call on different children. Ideas: *Local news, fun events in the community, accident reports, what's happening all over the world.*) Raise your hand if you can tell us a kind of music we hear on the radio. (Call on different children. Ideas: *Rock and roll, classical, country-western.*)

(Show children the page where the community is helping the family furnish their home. Point to the sign that says Rose's Pizza.) This sign says **Rose's Pizza.** What does this sign say? (Signal.) *Rose's Pizza.* Signs and billboards tell us information about things we can buy. What do signs and billboards tell us? (Signal.) *Information about things we can buy.* (Point to the signs in the window.) The two signs in the windows say **pizza** and **soda.** Do you think they sell pizza and soda in this store? (Signal.) *Yes.* How do you know they sell pizza and soda? (Call on a child. Idea: *It says pizza and soda on the signs in the windows.*)

Recalling Information

Let's remember some of the things we learned about *A Chair for My Mother,* and I'll write them down for you.

> **Note:** Use the cumulative wall chart started in Lesson 1 for recording information from the "Recalling Information" activity in this literature lesson.

What is the title of today's book? (Signal.) A Chair for My Mother. (Write the title on the chart.)

Who are the important characters in this story? (Call on different children. Ideas: *Girl, Mama, Grandma.* Write characters on chart.)

Tell me a word that describes each character. (Call on different children. Accept two words for each character. Record on chart.)

The setting of a story tells where and when the story happened. What does the setting of a story tell? (Signal.) *Where and when the story happened.* Where does this story take place? (Call on a child. Ideas: *Blue Tile Diner, home, furniture store, city.* Record on chart.)

When does this story take place? (Call on a child. Ideas: *Spring, one year.* Record on chart.)

What was the girl's problem in the story? (Call on a child. Ideas: *Their old house burned down. They didn't have a sofa or a big chair.* Record on chart.)

How did that problem make the girl feel? (Call on a child. Ideas: *Worried about her mother, upset.* Record on chart.)

How did the family attempt to solve its problem? (Call on a child. Idea: *They worked hard and saved their coins in a jar.* Record on chart.)

What was the solution to the family's problem? (Call on a child. Idea: *They saved enough money to buy a new chair.* Record on chart.)

Free Choice Reading Program (Lessons 2–19)

Introduce the children to the Free Choice Reading Program. This may be a designated shared reading time with a volunteer or older child, silent reading period of 15 minutes, or assigned as homework from reading resources other than the classroom reader. Self-closing, plastic shopping bags or zipping plastic bags work well as homework bags. A list of suggested books that correspond with a grade 2 reading level is provided at the end of this section.

(Show children a selection of books.) You are becoming very good readers. These are books that I think you can read by yourselves or with a little help. (Explain what your choice of routine is for this program. Explain any incentives you may be offering that will encourage children to get involved in reading)

Recommended Series

Easy

Hello Reader! Levels 2 and 3. Scholastic Inc., New York. Series of high-interest books with simple vocabulary and adjusted sentence length.

I Can Read Series. Levels 2 and 3. Harper Trophy: A Division of Harper Collins Publishers, USA. Short simple stories for the early reader. Wide variety of topics. Fiction and nonfiction.

Readers Club Story Books. J/P Associates, Valley Stream, New York. Simple phonetic stories. Also available as Blackline Masters.

Step into Reading Series. Steps 2 and 3. Random House, Inc. New York. Easy-to-read storybooks that are well-illustrated and interesting to the beginning reader.

Beginning Chapter Books

Cam Jansen Series. Adler, David A. A Puffin Book, New York. Mystery series featuring a girl detective named Cam. More difficult than Nate the Great.

Magic Treehouse Series. Osborne, Mary Pope. Scholastic, Inc., New York. A great adventure series that introduces various places and times in history. Web sites for additional children's activities are quoted at the backs of the books.

Marvin Redpost Series. Sachar, Louis. Random House, New York. Humorous stories about the adventures of Marvin, who believes that he was kidnapped at birth.

Nate the Great Series. Sharmat, Marjorie Weinman. A Dell Yearling, New York.

A simple mystery series with a child detective named Nate.

ADDITIONAL LITERATURE

Following are some additional titles that your students may enjoy during and following this lesson.

Tina's Diner by JoAnn Adinolfi

Cherries and Cherry Pits by Vera B. Williams

Music, Music for Everyone by Vera B. Williams

PARTS OF THE DICTIONARY

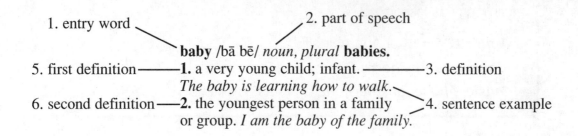

1. entry word
2. part of speech
5. first definition ——— **1.** a very young child; infant. ——— 3. definition
The baby is learning how to walk.
6. second definition ——— **2.** the youngest person in a family
4. sentence example
or group. *I am the baby of the family.*

DICTIONARY

add   **1**   **bring**

add /ad/ *verb* **add ed, add ing.**
1. to find the sum of two or more numbers. *If you add 2 and 7, you will get 9.* **2.** to put in or on as something extra. *We added a porch to our house.*

an i mals /an′ ə məlz/ *noun,* plural of **an i mal. 1.** living things that take in food, move about, and are made up of many cells.
2. living creatures other than humans. *My aunt and uncle raise animals on their farm.*

ants /ants/ *noun,* plural of **ant.** small insects related to bees and wasps. Ants live together in large groups called colonies.

a way /ə wā′/ *adjective* **1.** distance. *The town is 3 miles away.*
2. absent; somewhere else. *My cousin has gone away. —adverb* from this or that place. *The frightened rabbit hopped away from the dog.*

ba by /bā′ bē/ *noun, plural* **ba bies.**
1. a very young child; infant. *The baby is learning how to walk.*
2. the youngest person in a family or group. *I am the baby of the family.*

barn /bärn/ *noun, plural* **barns.** a building on a farm that is used to store hay and grain and to house cows and horses. *The cows stay in the barn when it is cold.*

bears /bârz/ *noun,* plural of **bear.** large, heavy animals with thick shaggy fur, sharp claws, and very short tails. Kinds of bears include black bears, brown bears, and polar bears.

bring /bring/ *verb* **brought, bring ing. 1.** to cause something or someone to come with you. *Remember to bring your book home.* **2.** to cause something to come or happen. *The heavy rains will bring floods.*

cane /kān/ *noun, plural* **canes.**
1. a stick used to help someone walk. *I need a cane to walk.*
2. another item shaped like such a stick. *I ate a candy cane.*

chick /chik/ *noun, plural* **chicks.**
1. a baby chicken. **2.** a baby bird.

clown /kloun/ *noun, plural* **clowns.**
a person who makes people laugh by playing tricks or doing stunts. A clown in a circus often wears funny clothing and makeup. *Clowns are funny.*

coal /kōl/ *noun, plural* **coals.** a fuel used to make heat and electricity.

could n't /kùd' ənt/ *contraction* for **could not.** *The puppy couldn't sit still.*

cows /kouz/ *noun,* plural of **cow.** the fully grown females of cattle. Cows are raised for their milk, meat, and hides.

did n't /did' ənt/ *contraction* for **did not.** *I didn't do my chores.*

dog house /dòg' hoùs'/ *noun, plural* **dog hous es.** a shelter built for a dog.

don't /dōnt/ *contraction* for **do not.** *Please don't be late.*

ducks /duks/ *noun,* plural of **duck.** waterbirds that have broad bills and webbed feet that help them swim.

eight /āt/ *noun, plural* **eights.** one more than seven; 8. *Will eight hot dogs be enough?*

eve ry where /ev' rē hwâr, ev' rē wâr'/ *adverb,* in every place; in all places. *Have you looked everywhere for the book you lost?*

fast /fast/ *adverb* **fast er, fast est.** moving quickly. *A fast train rushed by.*

find /fīnd/ *verb* **found, find ing.**
1. to discover or come upon by accident. *I found a wallet on the sidewalk.* **2.** to get or learn by thinking or working. *Please find the sum of this column of numbers.*

first /fûrst/ *adjective,* before all others. *George Washington was the first president of the United States.* —*adverb,* before all others. *She was ranked first in her class.*

fix /fiks/ *verb* **fixed, fix ing.**
1. to repair; mend. *I fixed the broken chair.* **2.** to get ready or arrange. *I will fix dinner.* —*noun, plural* **fix es.** trouble; bad place. *I got myself into quite a fix by promising to go to two parties on the same evening.*

fly /flī/ *verb* **flew, flown, fly ing.**
1. to move through the air with wings. *Some birds fly south for the winter.* **2.** to pilot or travel in

an aircraft. *The children flew to Puerto Rico to visit their grandparents.* **3.** to move, float. *I went to the park to fly my kite.*

found /found/ *verb,* past tense of **find.**

fu el /fyoo′ əl/ *noun, plural* **fu els.** something that provides heat and power. Coal, wood, and oil are fuels.

grass hop pers /gras′ hop′ ərz/ *noun,* insects that have wings and long, powerful legs that they use for jumping.

hat /hat/ *noun, plural* **hats.** a covering for the head.

hop /hop/ *verb* **hopped, hop ping. 1.** to make a short jump on one foot. **2.** to move by jumping on both feet or all feet at once. *The frog hopped from one lily pad to another.*

I'm /īm/ *contraction* for **I am.** *I'm going to the beach today.*

in side /in′ sīd′, in sīd′/ *noun, plural* **in sides.** the inner side or part; interior. *The inside of the house was dark.*

jog /jog/ *verb* **jogged, jog ging.** to run or move at a slow, steady pace. *My parents jog in the park every morning for exercise.* —*noun* the act of jogging. *She likes to take a jog in the park.*

jump /jump/ *verb* **jumped, jump ing.** to use a push from one's feet to move through or into the air. *He had to jump to catch the ball.*

knew /noo/ *verb,* past tense of **know.** to understand; was certain of the facts or truth.

last /last/ *adjective,* coming at the end. *The baby is the last one to go to sleep. I was the last person in line.*

let's /lets/ *contraction* for **let us.** *Let's go to the game.*

lose /looz/ *verb* **lost, los ing. 1.** to have no longer. *Did you lose your pencil?* **2.** to fail to win. *The team will lose the game.*

lost /lôst/ *verb,* past tense of **lose.** *I lost my gloves.*

lot /lot/ *noun, plural* **lots. 1.** a great amount. *There are a lot of cars on this road.* **2.** a piece of land. *We play baseball on an empty lot.*

lunch room /lunch′ room′, lunch′ room′/ *noun, plural* **lunch rooms.** a place where light meals are served, especially a cafeteria in a school.

man y /men′ ē/ *adjective* **more, most.** made up of a large number. *There are many books on American history.* —*noun,* a large number. *The meeting of the club was canceled because many of the members could not be there.*

mend /mend/ *verb* **mend ed, mend ing.** to put in good condition again. *Use glue to mend the dish.*

needs /nēdz/ *verb* a form of **need.** lacks or requires. *He needs a new coat.* —*noun plural of* **need.** requirements.

now /nou/ *adverb* **1.** at this time; at this moment. *My friends are at the beach now, while I'm here working.* **2.** without delay. *Eat your food now.*

one /wun/ *noun, plural* **ones.** the first and lowest number; 1.

out /out/ *adverb,* away from the center or from inside. *Water ran out when I turned on the faucet.*

poor /po͞or/ *adjective* **poor er, poor est.** having little money. *We are too poor to buy a boat.*

pull /po͝ol/ *verb* **pulled, pull ing.** to grab or hold something and move it forward or toward oneself. *Two horses pulled the wagon.*

push /po͝osh/ *verb* **pushed, push ing. 1.** to press on something in order to move it. *I pushed the cart through the market.* **2.** to move forward with effort. *We had to push through the crowd.*

quick /kwik/ *adjective* fast. *The quick fox jumped out of the way.*

rab bits /rab′ its/ *noun,* plural of **rabbit.** small animals that have long ears, a short tail, and soft fur. *Rabbits live in burrows that they dig in the ground.*

rich /rich/ *adjective* **rich er, rich est. 1.** having much money, land, or other valuable things. *The rich family gave a lot of money to charity.* **2.** having a lot of something. *Our country is rich in natural resources.*

ride /rīd/ *verb* **rode, rid den, rid ing.** to sit on and be carried by something that is moving, such as a horse. *I will ride a camel at the zoo.*

run /run/ *verb* **ran, run, run ning. 1.** to go or cause to go quickly. *I run really fast when I am scared.* **2.** duration, length. *The play will run for six weeks.*

sick /sik/ *adjective* **sick er, sick est.** poor health. *My friend is sick with a cold.*

slow /slō/ *adjective* **slow er, slow est. 1.** acting, moving, or happening with little speed. *The student was slow to answer the question.* **2.** behind the correct time. *Your watch is slow.*

small ish /smôl′ ish/ *adjective,* somewhat small. *I have rather smallish hands.*

some thing /sum′ thing′/ *adverb,* a little bit; somewhat. *Your house looks something like ours.* —*pronoun,* a thing that is not known or stated. *Something is wrong with our car.*

store /stor/ *noun, plural* **stores.** **1.** a place where goods are sold. *They went to the grocery store.* **2.** a supply of things put away for future use. *A store of firewood is in the garage.*

sun flow er /sun′ flou′ ər/ *noun, plural* **sun flow ers.** a large flower that grows on a tall plant. *A sunflower has a brown center and yellow petals.*

take /tāk/ *verb,* **took, tak en, tak ing. 1.** to get a hold of; grasp. *The student took a book from the shelf.* **2.** to capture or win by using force or skill. *My friend's painting took first prize.* **3.** to obtain; get. *The nurse took my temperature.* **4.** to carry with one; bring. *My parents took two suitcases on their trip.*

tap /tap/ *verb* **tapped, tap ping.** to hit or strike lightly. *I tapped out the beat to the music.*

team /tēm/ *noun, plural* **teams.** a group that plays, acts, or works together. *A team of scientists discovered a cure for the disease.*

thick /thik/ *adjective* **thick er, thick est. 1.** having much space between one side or surface and another. *The outside wall of the building is thick.* **2.** growing or being close; dense. *The fog was thickest near the river.*

thin /thin/ *adjective* **thin ner, thin nest.** having little space between one side or surface and the other; not thick. *The thin wrapping paper did not hide the title of the book.*

think /thingk/ *verb* **thought, think ing. 1.** to use the mind to form ideas or to make decisions. *Think carefully before you answer.* **2.** to have or form in the mind as an opinion, belief, or idea. *The teacher thought we were related.* **3.** to call to mind or remember. *I was thinking of my grandmother.*

thun der cloud /thun′ dər kloud′/ *noun, plural* **thun der clouds.** a dark cloud of great height that makes thunder and lightning.

tow /tō/ *verb* **towed, tow ing.** to pull; to pull along. *The tugboat had to tow the boat to shore.*

un cle /ung′ kəl/ *noun, plural* **un cles. 1.** the brother of one's mother or father; the husband of one's aunt. *My uncle will go with me.*

val ley /val′ ē/ *noun, plural*
val leys. an area of low land
between hills and mountains. *We
hiked along the river in the
valley.*

vi brate /vī′ brāt/ *verb* **vi brat ed,
vi brat ing.** to move rapidly;
shake. *The strings of a guitar
vibrate when they are played.*

week end /wēk′ end′/ *noun, plural*
week ends. the period of time
from Friday night or Saturday
morning until Sunday night or
Monday morning. *We went to the
country for the weekend.*

west /west/ *noun* the direction
where the sun sets. *Look to the
west to see the beautiful sunset.*

wheel /hwēl, wēl/ *noun, plural*
wheels. a round frame or solid
object used on cars and wagons.
The car has four wheels.

why /hwī, wī/ *adverb,* for what
reason or purpose. *Why are you
laughing?*

wind[1] /wind/ *noun, plural* **winds.**
air moving over the ground. *The
wind blew the tree over.*

wind[2] /wīnd/ *verb* **wound,
wind ing. 1.** to roll into a ball.
I will wind this wool into a ball.
2. to turn in one direction or
another. *The road winds around
the mountain.*

wish /wish/ *noun, plural* **wish es.
1.** a feeling of wanting
something; a strong desire. **2.** a
thing that a person wants. *I hoped
for a compass for my birthday,
and I got my wish.*
—*verb* **wished, wish ing.** to want
something very much; have a
wish. *I wish that summer would
last longer.*

won't /wōnt/ contraction for **will
not.** *We won't fly in an airplane
today.*

x-ray /eks′ rā′/ *verb,* to examine or
photograph with x rays. *The
doctor will x-ray the girl's leg.*

yard /yärd/ *noun, plural* **yards.** an
area of ground next to or around
a house, school, or other
building. *We have a vegetable
garden in the yard around our
house.*

zoo /zo͞o/ *noun, plural* **zoos.** a park
or public place where wild
animals are kept for people to
see. *The children went to the zoo
to see the animals.*

Lesson 3

Language Skill Development

Alphabet Review/Parts of the Dictionary/Dictionary Skills

> **Time Required:** 30 minutes
> **Materials Required:** BLM 2A to 2F, one copy for each child (dictionary)
> BLM 3, one copy for each child

> **Note:** Refer to a poster or banner of the alphabet displayed prominently in the classroom for the alphabet review. Children may also review by singing the *Alphabet Song.*

How are the words in a dictionary listed? (Signal.) *In alphabetical order.* What order do words listed alphabetically follow? (Signal.) *The letters in the alphabet.*

What letters are the first part of the alphabet? (Signal.) *A, b, c, d, e, f, and g.* What letters are the middle part of the alphabet? (Signal.) *H, i, j, k, l, m, n, o, p, q, r, s, and t.* What letters are the last part of the alphabet? (Signal.) *U, v, w, x, y, and z.*

(Give a copy of the dictionary to each child.) Everybody, touch the words at the top of page 1 in your dictionary. (Check.) This says **Parts of the Dictionary.** What does this say? (Signal.) *Parts of the dictionary.*

Touch item number 1 in the dictionary example. (Check.) What does this say? (Signal.) *Entry word.* How is the entry word written? (Signal.) *With bold, dark letters.* The entry word shows how to spell the word. What does the entry word show? (Signal.) *How to spell the word.*

What is the entry word for this example? (Signal.) *Baby.* Raise your hand if you can tell us how to spell **baby** by looking at the bold entry word. (Call on a child.) *B-a-b-y.*

Touch item number 2 in the dictionary example. (Check.) What does this say? (Signal.) *Part of speech.* What does the part of speech tell you? (Signal.) *What kind of word it is.* You will learn more about parts of speech later this year.

Touch item number 3 in the dictionary example. (Check.) What does this say? (Signal.) *Definition.* What does the definition tell you? (Signal.) *What the word means.* Read the definition for the entry word **baby.** (Signal.) *A very young child; infant.* What is a **baby**? (Signal.) *A very young child; infant.*

Touch item number 4 in the dictionary example. (Check.) What does this say? (Signal.) *Sentence example.* What does the sentence example show you? (Signal.) *How to use the entry word in a sentence.* The sentence example is written in italics. How is the sentence example written? (Signal.) *In italics.* Read the sentence example for the entry word **baby.** (Signal.) *The baby is learning how to walk.*

Listen. Sometimes a word means more than one thing. Can a word sometimes mean more than one thing? (Signal.) *Yes.* Touch item number 5 in the dictionary example. (Check.) What does the bold number 1 tell you? (Signal.) *The first thing that the word means.* Raise your hand if you can remember the first definition of the word **baby.** (Call on a child. Idea: *A very young child; infant.*)

Touch item number 6 in the dictionary example. (Check.) What does the bold number 2 tell you? (Signal.) *The second thing that the entry word means.* Read the second definition for the entry word **baby.** (Signal.) *The youngest person in a family or group.* What is the second thing that **baby** means? (Signal.) *The youngest person in a family or group.*

Touch the sentence example for the second definition of the word **baby** in italics. (Check.) Read the sentence example for the second definition of the word **baby.** (Signal.) *I am the baby of the family.*

Guide Words/ Word Search

Now touch the word **Dictionary** under the example. (Check.) This is where your dictionary begins. The words listed in a dictionary are written in two columns. How are the words listed in a dictionary written? (Signal.) *In two columns.*

Touch the bold word at the top of the first column on page 1. (Check.) This bold word is called a **guide word.** What is this word called? (Signal.) *A guide word.* This guide word at the top of the left-hand column tells you which entry word is listed **first** on the page. What does the guide word at the top of the left-hand column tell you? (Signal.) *Which entry word is listed first on the page.* Raise your hand if you would like to read this guide word to the class. (Call on a child.) *Add.* What letter does **add** begin with? (Signal.) *A.*

Touch the first bold entry word in the first column. Read the word. (Signal.) *Add.* Is this the same word as the guide word written above it? (Signal.) *Yes.* This is the first word beginning with the letter **a** listed in your dictionary.

Let's read the first definition for the word **add** together. (Signal.) *To find the sum of two or more numbers.* Read the first sentence example for the word **add.** (Signal.) *If you add 2 and 7, you will get 9.* (Repeat for the second definition.)

Touch the bold word at the top of the second column on page 1. (Check.) This bold word is also a guide word. This guide word at the top of the right-hand column tells you which entry word is listed **last** on the page. What does the guide word at the top of the right-hand column tell you? (Signal.) *Which entry word is listed last on the page.* Raise your hand if you would like to read this guide word to the class. (Call on a child.) *Bring.* What letter does **bring** begin with? (Signal.) *B.*

Touch the last bold entry word at the bottom of the second column. (Check.) Let's read this word together. (Signal.) *Bring.* Is this the same word as the guide word written at the top of the right-hand column on this page? (Signal.) *Yes.* **Bring** is the last word on this page of the dictionary beginning with the letter **b.**

Read the first definition for the word **bring.** (Signal.) *To cause something or someone to come with you.* Is there a sentence example for this word? (Signal.) *Yes.* Read the sentence example for the first definition of **bring.** (Signal.) *Remember to bring your book home.*

Look in the first column of your dictionary. Raise your hand if you can tell us another word that begins with the letter **a.** (Call on different children. Accept correct responses. Read the definitions and the sentence examples for each word.)

Look in the second column of your dictionary. Raise your hand if you can tell us the first word that begins with the letter **b.** (Call on a child.) *Baby.* Does the letter **b** come after the letter **a** in the alphabet? (Signal.) *Yes.* Do the words beginning with the letter **b** come after the words beginning with the letter **a** in the dictionary? (Signal.) *Yes.* Raise your hand if you can tell us another word that begins with the letter **b.** (Call on different children. Accept correct responses. Read the definitions and the sentence examples for each word.)

Turn to page 2 of your dictionary. Look in the first column on page 2. Raise your hand if you can tell us the first word that begins with the letter **c.** (Call on a child.) *Cane.* Does the letter **c** come after the letter **b** in the alphabet? (Signal.) *Yes.* Do the words beginning with the letter **c** come after the words beginning with the letter **b** in the dictionary? (Signal.) *Yes.* Raise your hand if you can tell us another word that begins with the letter **c.** (Call on different children. Accept correct responses. Read the definitions and the sentence examples for each word.)

(Repeat process for the second column on page 2, and for both columns on page 3 of the dictionary.)

Worksheet

Now, you will practice putting words into alphabetical order. What will you practice? (Signal.) *Putting words into alphabetical order.* To put words into alphabetical order, you use the same order as the letters of the alphabet. To put words into alphabetical order, what do you use? (Signal.) *The same order as the letters of the alphabet.*

(Hand out a copy of BLM 3 to each child.) Look at the first letter of each word in the box. Put the words in alphabetical order on the lines below. You can use your dictionaries to help you.

Technology

Children may use children's dictionary software for practice using another format of dictionary.

Literature

Dancing with the Indians

by Angela Shelf Medearis

Illustrated by Samuel Byrd

Prereading

Examining the Book

This is the book that I am going to share with you today. The title of this book is *Dancing with the Indians.* What's the title of today's book? (Signal.) Dancing with the Indians.

The author of this story is Angela Shelf Medearis. Who is the author of *Dancing with the Indians*? (Signal.) *Angela Shelf Medearis.*

The illustrator of this book is Samuel Byrd. Who is the illustrator of *Dancing with the Indians*? (Signal.) *Samuel Byrd.*

Making Predictions

> **Note:** Many of the activities in this literature program depend on children examining the outside cover of the book. Make an effort to obtain a copy with a dustcover or illustration on the front and back. If this is not possible, use the illustration on the title page of the picture book, if there is one. The first illustration in the story may also be used for making predictions.

When we tell what we think the story is about we are making a prediction. What are we doing when we tell what we think the story is about? (Signal.) *Making a prediction.*

(Show the children the front and back covers of the book.) Look at the front and back covers. Raise your hand if you can ask a **who** question that will help us make predictions about this story. (Call on a child. Ideas: *Who is the story about? Who is in the picture?* Call on one or two different children to answer the question asked.) Raise your hand if you can ask a **what** question that will help us make predictions about this story. (Call on a child. Ideas: *What are they doing? What do you see?* Call on one or two different children to answer the question asked.) Raise your hand if you can ask a **where** question that will help us make predictions about this story. (Call on a child. Idea: *Where are they?* Call on one or two different children to answer the question asked.)

Reading the Story

I'm going to read the story aloud to you and show you the pictures. After I read the story to you, we will talk about the story. (Read the story with minimal interruptions. This ensures that the children hear the story in its entirety, thus helping them develop a better sense of story. Occasionally you may find it beneficial to discuss parts of the story that are complicated or have unfamiliar vocabulary. Encourage children to check the illustrations, the structures of words, and context to help them decipher unknown words and their meanings.)

Discussing the Book

Story Pattern

Most books have a pattern. Let's see if we can figure out the pattern for this book. You tell me what happened in the story and I'll write it on the chalkboard.

> **Note:** As the children retell the story, make a story map of the main story events on the chalkboard similar to the sample in Lesson 1. (Discuss the sequence of story events briefly to construct the story map.)

(Point to the story map that is on the chalkboard.) Look at the shape of this story. This story starts and ends with a family riding across a field in a horse-drawn cart. What's the pattern for this story? (Signal.) *A circle.*

Characters and Setting

All stories have a beginning, a middle, and an ending. The word **character** tells who is in the story. What does the word **character** tell? (Signal.) *Who is in the story.* The beginning of a story tells about the characters that are in the story. What does the beginning of a story tell about? (Signal.) *The characters that are in the story.* Who are the important characters in *Dancing with the Indians*? (Call on different children. Ideas: *Grandpa, the girl, Mama, the Seminole Indians.*)

The beginning also tells about the setting of the story. The setting tells where and when the story happens. What does the setting tell? (Signal.) *Where and when the story happens.* Where does this story happen? (Call on a child. Ideas: *In the country, at the Seminole village.*) When does this story happen? (Call on a child. Idea: *At night.*)

Poetry

This book is special because it is a poem. Most books use sentences and paragraphs to tell the story. What do most books use to tell a story? (Signal.) *Sentences and paragraphs.* Poems and songs are different. They use lines and verses instead of sentences and paragraphs. What do poems and songs use instead of sentences and paragraphs? (Signal.) *Lines and verses.*

(Copy onto the chalkboard the verse from the first page of the ribbon dance and the verse where the dancers join their hands. Point to the first verse.) How many lines are there in this verse? (Signal.) *Four.* (Point to the second verse.) How many lines are there in this verse? (Signal.) *Four.*

Using lines and verses is one thing that makes poems special. Another thing that is special about poems is that they often use words that rhyme. What is another thing that makes poems special? (Signal.) *Words that rhyme.* Sometimes writers make the last words of different lines rhyme so that the poem is more fun to read.

(Point to the last word of the first line of the first verse on the chalkboard.) What does this word say? (Signal.) *First.* (Write the letter **A** beside this line. Point to the last word of line two.) What does this word say? (Signal.) *Around.* Do the last words of the first and second lines rhyme? (Signal.) *No.* (Write the letter **B** beside this line.)

(Point to the last word of the third line.) What does this word say? (Signal.) *Ankles.* (Point to each line.) Do the last words of the first and third lines rhyme? (Signal.) *No.* (Point to each line.) Do the last words of the second and third lines rhyme? (Signal.) *No.* (Write the letter **C** beside this line.)

(Point to the last word of the fourth line.) What does this word say? (Signal.) *Sound.* (Point to each line.) Do the last words of the first and fourth lines rhyme? (Signal.) *No.* Do the last words of the second and fourth lines rhyme? (Signal.) *Yes.* Do the last words of the third and fourth lines rhyme? (Signal.) *No.* What letter is written beside the second line? (Signal.) *B.* (Write the letter **B** beside the last line.)

The rhyming pattern for this verse is ABCB. What's the rhyming pattern for this verse? (Signal.) *ABCB.* (Repeat this process with the second verse on the chalkboard.) Is the rhyming pattern the same in the first and second verses? (Signal.) *Yes.* All of the verses in this book follow this same rhyming pattern.

Note: On the last page of this book, the author has written a summary of her family's history. As an optional activity, you may wish to read and discuss this section with the children.

Illustrations

Let's look at the illustrations that Samuel Byrd made. Samuel Byrd used a combination of many different techniques to make his drawings. He used watercolors, crayons, and ink. What did Samuel Byrd use to make the illustrations in *Dancing with the Indians*? (Signal.) *Watercolors, crayons, and ink.*

Recalling Information

Let's remember some of the things that we learned about *Dancing with the Indians,* and I'll write them down for you.

Note: Use the cumulative wall chart started in Lesson 1 for recording information from the "Recalling Information" activity in this literature lesson.

What is the title of today's book? (Signal.) Dancing with the Indians. (Write the title on the chart.)

Who are the important characters in this story? (Call on different children. Ideas: *Girl, Mama, Grandpa.* Record on chart.)

Tell me a word that describes each character. (Call on different children. Accept two words for each character. Record on chart.)

The setting of a story tells where and when the story happened. What does the setting of a story tell? (Signal.) *Where and when the story happened.* Where does this story take place? (Call on a child. Ideas: *In the country, at the Seminole village.* Record on chart.)

When does this story take place? (Call on a child. Idea: *At night.* Record on chart.)

The characters in this story didn't have a problem, so we will leave the rest of the squares blank.

Technology

(To give children practice with rhyming, you may use beginning reading and phonics programs that contain rhyming activities that can be completed on the computer.)

ADDITIONAL LITERATURE

Following are some additional titles that your students may enjoy during and following this lesson.

Daisy and the Doll by Angela Shelf Medearis

Annie's Gifts by Angela Shelf Medearis

Rum-A-Tum-Tum by Angela Shelf Medearis

Look at the first letter of each word in the box. Put the words in alphabetical order on the lines below. You can use your dictionaries to help you.

1.

| valley | ride | hop |

_____ _____ _____

2.

| last | bears | cows |

_____ _____ _____

3.

| X-ray | wish | one |

_____ _____ _____

4.

| needs | ducks | quick |

_____ _____ _____

5.

| eight | hat | zoo |

_____ _____ _____

6.

| wheel | now | rabbits |

_____ _____ _____

7.

| cane | animals | slow |

_____ _____ _____

Lesson 4

Language Skill Development

Alphabet Review/Parts of the Dictionary

Title: *Dictionary Skills*

Time Required: 15 minutes

Materials Required: Dictionary made from BLMs in Lesson 2, one copy for each child

Today you will review how to use a dictionary. How are the words in a dictionary listed? (Signal.) *In alphabetical order.* What order do words listed alphabetically follow? (Signal.) *The letters in the alphabet.*

What letters are in the first part of the alphabet? (Signal.) *A, b, c, d, e, f, and g.* What letters are in the middle part of the alphabet? (Signal.) *H, i, j, k, l, m, n, o, p, q, r, s, and t.* What letters are in the last part of the alphabet? (Signal.) *U, v, w, x, y, and z.*

(Give a copy of the dictionary to each child.) Everybody, touch the words at the top of page 1 in your dictionary. (Check.) What does this say? (Signal.) *Parts of the dictionary.*

Touch item number 1 in the dictionary example. (Check.) What does this say? (Signal.) *Entry word.* How is the entry word written? (Signal.) *With bold, dark letters.* What does the entry word show? (Signal.) *How to spell the word.*

The entry word for this example is **baby.** What is the entry word for this example? (Signal.) *Baby.* Raise your hand if you can tell us how to spell **baby** by looking at the bold entry word. (Call on a child.) *B-a-b-y.*

Touch item number 2 in the dictionary example. (Check.) This says **part of speech.** What does this say? (Signal.) *Part of speech.* What does the part of speech tell you? (Signal.) *What kind of word it is.* You will learn more about parts of speech later this year.

Touch item number 3 in the dictionary example. (Check.) What does this say? (Signal.) *Definition.* What does the definition tell you? (Signal.) *What the word means.* Read the definition for the entry word **baby.** (Signal.) *A very young child; infant.* What is a **baby**? (Signal.) *A very young child; infant.*

Touch item number 4 in the dictionary example. (Check.) What does this say? (Signal.) *Sentence example.* What does the sentence example show you? (Signal.) *How to use the entry word in a sentence.* How is the sentence example written? (Signal.) *In italics.* Read the sentence example for the entry word **baby.** (Signal.) *The baby is learning how to walk.*

Can a word sometimes mean more than one thing? (Signal.) *Yes.* Touch item number 5 in the dictionary example. (Check.) What is this? (Signal.) *A bold number 1.* What does the bold number 1 tell you? (Signal.) *The first thing that the word means.* Raise your hand if you can remember the first definition of the word **baby**. (Call on a child. Idea: *A very young child; infant.*)

Touch item number 6 in the dictionary example. (Check.) What is this? (Signal.) *A bold number 2.* What does the bold number 2 tell you? (Signal.) *The second thing that the entry word means.* Read the second definition for the entry word **baby**. (Signal.) *The youngest person in a family or group.* What is the second thing that **baby** means? (Signal.) *The youngest person in a family or group.*

Touch the sentence example for the second definition of the word **baby** in italics. (Check.) Read the sentence example for the second meaning of the word **baby.** (Signal.) *I am the baby of the family.*

Guide Words/Word Search

How many columns are used to list words in a dictionary? (Signal.) *Two columns.*

Touch the bold word at the top of the first column on page 4. (Check.) What is this word called? (Signal.) *A guide word.* What does the guide word at the top of the left-hand column tell you? (Signal.) *Which entry word is listed first on the page.* Read the guide word. (Signal.) *Mend.* What letter does **mend** begin with? (Signal.) *M.*

Touch the first bold entry word in the first column. Read the word. (Signal.) *Mend.* Is this the same word as the guide word written above it? (Signal.) *Yes.* **Mend** is the first word beginning with the letter **m** on this page in your dictionary.

Read the first definition for the word **mend**. (Signal.) *To put in good condition again.* Read the first sentence example for the word **mend**. (Signal.) *Use glue to mend the dish.*

Touch the bold word at the top of the second column on page 4. (Check.) What is this bold word called? (Signal.) *A guide word.* What does the guide word at the top of the right-hand column tell you? (Signal.) *Which entry word is listed last on the page.* Read the guide word. (Signal.) *Smallish.* What letter does **smallish** begin with? (Signal.) *S.*

Touch the last bold entry word at the bottom of the second column. (Check.) Read the entry word. (Signal.) *Smallish.* Is this the same word as the guide word written at the top of this column? (Signal.) *Yes.* **Smallish** is the last word on this page of the dictionary beginning with the letter **s.**

Read the first definition for the word **smallish.** (Signal.) *Somewhat small.* Read the sentence example for this word. (Signal.) *I have rather smallish hands.*

Look in the first column on page 5. Raise your hand if you can tell us another word that begins with the letter **s.** (Call on different children. Accept correct responses. Read the definitions and the sentence examples for each word.)

Look in the first column on page 5. Raise your hand if you can tell us the first word that begins with the letter **t.** (Call on a child. *Take.*) Read the first definition for the word **take.** (Signal.) *To get a hold of; grasp.* Is there a sentence example for the word **take**? (Signal.) *Yes.* Read the sentence example for the first definition. (Signal.) *The student took a book from the shelf.* (Repeat process for the word beginning with **u.**)

Look on page 6 of your dictionary. Raise your hand if you can tell us the first word that begins with the letter **v.** (Call on a child. *Valley.*) Does the letter **v** come after the letter **u** in the alphabet? (Signal.) *Yes.* Do the words beginning with the letter **v** come after the words beginning with the letter **u** in the dictionary? (Signal.) *Yes.* Raise your hand if you can tell us another word that begins with the letter **v**. (Call on a child. *Vibrate.*) Read the definition of the word **vibrate.** (Signal.) *To move rapidly; shake.* Is there a sentence example for the word **vibrate**? (Signal.) *Yes.* Read the sentence example for **vibrate.** (Signal.) *The strings of a guitar vibrate when they are plucked.* (Repeat process for words beginning with **w, x, y,** and **z.**)

(Repeat process for other pages of the dictionary.)

Worksheet

Now you will practice putting words into alphabetical order. What will you practice? (Signal.) *Putting words into alphabetical order.* To put words into alphabetical order, you use the same order as the letters of the alphabet. To put words into alphabetical order, what do you use? (Signal.) *The same order as the letters of the alphabet.*

(Hand a copy of BLM 4 to each child.) Look at the first and second letters of each word in the box. Put the words in alphabetical order on the lines below. You can use your dictionaries to help you.

Technology

Children may use children's dictionary software for practice using another format of dictionary.

Literature

Grandfather's Journey

by Allen Say

Prereading

Examining the Book

This is the next book that I am going to share with you. The title of this book is *Grandfather's Journey.* What's the title of today's book? (Signal.) Grandfather's Journey.

Sometimes the same person writes the story and makes the pictures. Sometimes the author and illustrator are two different people. Allen Say wrote this story and he made the pictures. Did the same person write the story and make the pictures for

Grandfather's Journey? (Signal.) *Yes.* Allen Say is both the author and the illustrator of this book. Who is the author of *Grandfather's Journey?* (Signal.) *Allen Say.* Who is the illustrator of *Grandfather's Journey?* (Signal.) *Allen Say.*

Making Predictions

(Assign each child a partner. Show children the front and back covers of the book.) Look at the front and back covers. Tell your partner what you think the story will be about. (Allow about one minute for sharing predictions.)

Raise your hand if you would like to tell us your prediction of what you think the story will be about. (Call on three different children. Accept reasonable responses.)

Reading the Story

I'm going to read the story aloud to you and show you the pictures. After I read the story to you, we will talk about the story. (Read the story with minimal interruptions.)

Discussing the Book

Story Pattern

Most books have a pattern. Let's see if we can figure out the pattern for this book. You tell me what happened in the story and I'll write it on the chalkboard.

Note: As the children retell the story, make a story map of the main story events on the chalkboard similar to the sample in Lesson 2.

(Discuss the sequence of story events briefly to construct the story map.)

(Point to the story map that is on the chalkboard.) Look at the shape of this story. This story starts and ends in different places. What do we call a story that starts and ends in different places? (Signal.) *A linear story.*

Characters and Setting

All stories have a beginning, a middle, and an ending. The beginning of a story tells about the characters that are in the story. What does the beginning of a story tell about? (Signal.) *The characters that are in the story.* Who is the most important character in *Grandfather's Journey?* (Call on different children. Idea: *Grandfather.*)

The beginning also tells about the setting of the story. What does the setting tell? (Signal.) *Where and when the story happens.* What country does Grandfather leave at the beginning of the story? (Signal.) *Japan.* Where is Grandfather at the end of the story? (Signal.) *North America.*

(Show children page 9.) What do you see in this picture that tells in what time of year this part of the story takes place? (Call on different children. Ideas: *Sunshine, tall yellow grass, the boy isn't wearing his jacket.*) Tall yellow grass grows only in late summer, so we know that this part of the story takes place during late summer. When does this part of the story take place? (Signal.) *In late summer.*

Story Problem

A story often has a problem that changes the everyday life of at least one of the characters. What was Grandfather's problem? (Call on a child. Ideas: *He was homesick for Japan. He missed his old friends.*)

In stories with a problem, the problem changes the feelings of the characters, so they decide to do something about the problem. How did Grandfather feel about his problem? (Call on a child. Idea: *Sad, lonely.*)

The middle of a story tells what the character does to try to solve a problem. This is called the attempt at solution. What did Grandfather decide to do about his problem? (Call on a child. Idea: *He took his family back to Japan.*)

Raise your hand if you can tell us what Grandfather did to solve his problem after the war destroyed his city house. (Call on a child. Idea: *The family returned to the village where they grew up.*)

The end of the story tells what happened to solve the final problem. This is called the solution to the problem. What did Grandfather want to see so badly one more time? (Signal.) *California.* Did he ever get to see California? (Signal.) *No.* Did his grandson see California? (Signal.) *Yes.* The grandson solved Grandfather's problem by going to see California himself. How did the grandson solve the problem of Grandfather missing California? (Signal.) *He saw California himself.*

Raise your hand if you can tell us a problem the grandson had. (Call on different children. Ideas: *He misses the mountains and rivers where he grew up. He misses his old friends. He's homesick.*) What does he do to solve his problem? (Call on a child. Idea: *He travels back and forth between California and Japan.*)

Illustrations

(Point to the medal on the front cover.) This book is special because it won first prize for its pictures. This prize it won is called the Caldecott Medal. Raise your hand if you can tell us the name of another book we read that won this prize. (Call on a child.) A Chair for My Mother. (Show children the cover of *A Chair for My Mother.*) What color is the medal? (Signal.) *Silver.* (Show the cover of *Grandfather's Journey.*) What color is the medal? (Signal.) *Gold.* Which color medal do you think is for first prize? (Signal.) *Gold.* Which color medal do you think is for second prize? (Signal.) *Silver.*

Let's look at the illustrations that Allen Say made. There are many different ways to make illustrations for a book: you can paint them; you can draw them with a pen or pencil; you can make them with markers, crayons, or chalk. How do you think Allen Say made his illustrations? (Call on a child. Idea: *Watercolors.*)

(Show children the last illustration in the book.) What is this kind of picture called? (Signal.) *A portrait.* This family portrait is a watercolor painting. What else could you use to show a family portrait? (Call on a child. Idea: *A camera to take a photograph.*) The illustrator shows this family portrait glued into a frame. Raise your hand if you can tell us about places where you see portraits in a frame. (Call on different children. Accept reasonable responses.)

Recalling Information

Let's remember some of the things we learned about *Grandfather's Journey,* and I'll write them down for you.

Note: Use the cumulative wall chart started in Lesson 1 for recording information from the "Recalling Information" activity in this literature lesson.

What is the title of today's book? (Signal.) Grandfather's Journey. (Write the title on the chart.)

Who are the important characters in this story? (Call on different children. Ideas: *Grandfather, his wife, his daughter, his grandson.* Record on chart.)

Tell me a word that describes each character. (Call on different children. Accept two words for each character. Record on chart.)

Where does this story take place? (Call on a child. Ideas: *Japan, North America, California.* Record on chart.) When does this story take place? (Call on a child. Ideas: *Spring, summer, during Grandfather's lifetime.* Record on chart.)

What was Grandfather's problem in the story? (Call on a child. Ideas: *He was homesick. He missed his friends.* Record on chart.)

How did that problem make Grandfather feel? (Call on a child. Idea: *Sad, lonely.* Record on chart.)

How did Grandfather attempt to solve his problem? (Call on a child. Idea: *He moved back to Japan.* Record on chart.)

What was the grandson's problem in the story? (Call on a child. Ideas: *He was homesick. He missed his friends.* Record on chart.)

How did that problem make the grandson feel? (Call on a child. Ideas: *Sad, lonely.* Record on chart.)

How did the grandson attempt to solve his problem? (Call on a child. Idea: *He traveled back and forth between California and Japan.*)

Reader Preference

(Point to the titles of the stories listed on the cumulative class chart.) We have read many stories that are listed on this chart. I'm going to read the title of each story. I want you to think about each story and pick out the one that is your favorite—the one that you liked best. (Point to and read aloud the title of each story.)

Raise your hand if you liked *Dumpling Soup* the best. (Remind children that they can vote only once.) Tell me why you liked this story the best. (Call on different children. Accept one reason from each child. Repeat process for *A Chair for My Mother.*)

The first two books are written as stories, but *Dancing with the Indians* is written as poetry. How is *Dancing with the Indians* written? (Signal.) *As poetry.* Raise your hand if you liked *Dancing with the Indians* best. Tell me why you liked this story the best. (Call on different children. Accept one reason for each child. Repeat process for *Grandfather's Journey.*)

ADDITIONAL LITERATURE

Following are some additional titles that your students may enjoy during and following this lesson.

Song and Dance Man by Karen Ackerman

The Lotus Seed by Sherry Garland

Knots on a Counting Rope by Bill Martin Jr. and John Archambault

1. | away   ants   add |

_____   _____

2. | store   small   sick |

_____   _____   _____

3. | clown   chick   coal |

_____   _____   _____

4. | tap   think   team |

_____   _____   _____

5. | fuel   fly   fast |

_____   _____   _____

6. | why   west   wish |

_____   _____   _____

Lesson 5

Language Skill Development

Proofreading for a capital at the beginning of a sentence, a period at the end, capital on the word **I** and on names.

Time Required: 30 minutes

Preparation: Print paragraph on the chalkboard: clouds tell you that it is
going to rain mike and
jan looked at the sky
don and i looked too
it began to rain

Make a class chart titled: Proofreading Marks

Note: Add to the Proofreading Marks chart each time you introduce a new proofreading mark.

Today you are going to learn about fixing sentences and words. When we fix a sentence or word, it is called **proofreading.** What do we call it when we fix a sentence or word? (Signal.) *Proofreading.*

Before you proofread some sentences, you need to learn some rules about sentences. Here's the first rule about sentences. Sentences start with a capital letter. How do sentences start? (Signal.) *With a capital letter.* (Point to the first sentence of the paragraph.)

This is a paragraph about rain. I'll read the first sentence. (Touch under the words as you read.) Clouds tell you that it is going to rain. Read the first sentence. (Signal.) *Clouds tell you that it is going to rain.* Raise your hand if you can tell us what needs fixing. (Call on a child. *It needs a capital letter at the beginning.*) I draw three little lines under the **c** in **cloud.** (Draw the lines.) This tells me to remember to put a capital letter at the beginning of this sentence when I copy it. What do three little lines tell me to remember? (Signal.) *To put a capital letter.* (Repeat process for each sentence.)

Here's the next rule about sentences. Sentences end with a period. How do sentences end? (Signal.) *With a period.* Read the first sentence. (Signal.) *Clouds tell you that it is going to rain.* Raise your hand if you can tell us what needs fixing. (Call on a child. *It needs a period at the end.*) I draw a circle with a period inside. (Draw a circle with a period inside after **rain.**) This tells me to remember to put a period at the end of this sentence when I copy it. What does a period inside a circle tell me to remember? (Signal.) *To put a period.* (Repeat process for each sentence.)

Here's a rule about words. A person's name starts with a capital letter. How does a person's name start? (Signal.) *With a capital letter.* (Point to the sentence that starts with

mike.) Read this sentence. (Signal.) *Mike and jan looked at the sky.* Raise your hand if you can tell us what needs fixing. (Call on a child. *The names mike and jan need capital letters.*) What do I write to help me remember to put a capital letter? (Signal.) *Three little lines.*

Here's a rule about words. The word **I** as in **I am your teacher** always needs a capital letter. What does the word **I** as in **I am your teacher** always need? (Signal.) *A capital letter.* (Point to the sentence that starts with **don.**) Read this sentence. (Signal.) *Don and i looked too.* Raise your hand if you can tell us what needs fixing. (Call on a child. *The words **I** and **Don** need capital letters.*) What do I write to help me remember to put a capital letter? (Signal.) *Three little lines.*

(Record proofreading marks learned in this lesson on class chart titled "Proofreading Marks." Have children copy the paragraph correctly onto paper or into a notebook. Make sure that children use the proofreading marks as reminders for correct usage and don't use them in their copy work. You may wish to repeat this part of the lesson as a short exercise three more times to reinforce and practice the skills taught.)

Literature

Birdie's Lighthouse

by Deborah Hopkinson

Illustrated by Kimberly Bulcken Root

Prereading

Examining the Book

This is the next book that I am going to share with you. The title of this book is *Birdie's Lighthouse*. What's the title of today's book? (Signal.) Birdie's Lighthouse.

The author of this story is Deborah Hopkinson. Who is the author of *Birdie's Lighthouse*? (Signal.) *Deborah Hopkinson.*

The illustrator of this book is Kimberly Bulcken Root. Who is the illustrator of *Birdie's Lighthouse*? (Signal.) *Kimberly Bulcken Root.*

Making Predictions

(Show the children the front and back covers of the book.) Look at the front and back covers. Raise your hand if you can ask a **who** question that will help us make predictions about this story. (Call on a child. Ideas: *Who is the girl? Who lives in the lighthouse?*

Who is Birdie?) Raise your hand if you can ask a **what** question that will help us make predictions about this story. (Call on a child. Ideas: *What are lighthouses for? What is the girl doing? What does the girl see?*) Raise your hand if you can ask a **where** question that will help us make predictions about this story. (Call on a child. Ideas: *Where is the lighthouse? Where does the story take place?*)

Reading the Story

I'm going to read the story aloud to you, and show you the pictures. After I read the story to you, we will talk about the story. (Read the story with minimal interruptions.)

Discussing the Book

Story Pattern

Most books have a pattern. Let's see if we can figure out the pattern for this book. You tell me what happened in the story and I'll write it on the chalkboard.

Note: As the children retell the story, make a story map of the main story events on the chalkboard similar to the sample in Lesson 2.

(Discuss the sequence of story events briefly to construct the story map.)

(Point to the story map that is on the chalkboard.) What's the pattern for this story? (Signal.) *Linear.*

(Show the children the first page of the story. Point to the year written at the top of the page.) Raise your hand if you can tell me what year this says. (Call on a child. *1855.*) (Point to **January 15.**) This says **January 15.** The date at the beginning of this story is January 15, 1855. What is the date at the beginning of this story? (Signal.) *January 15, 1855.*

(Show children the last page of the story. Point to the year written at the top of the page.) Raise your hand if you can tell me what year this says. (Call on a child. *1856.*) (Point to **January 15.**) This says **January 15.** The date at the end of this story is January 15, 1856. What is the date at the end of this story? (Signal.) *January 15, 1856.* (Point to the beginning of the story map on the chalkboard.) This story begins on January 15, 1855, and ends one year later. (Point to the end of the story map on the chalkboard.) on January 15, 1856. Does this story start and end in the same place? (Signal.) *No.* What's the pattern for this story? (Signal.) *A linear story.*

Characters and Setting

All stories have a beginning, a middle, and an ending. The beginning of a story tells about the characters that are in the story. What does the beginning of a story tell about? (Signal.) *The characters that are in the story.* Who are the important characters in *Birdie's Lighthouse*? (Call on different children. Ideas: *Bertha Holland or Birdie, Papa, Mama, Nate, Janey.*)

The beginning also tells about the setting of the story. Where does this story happen? (Call on a child. Ideas: *In a lighthouse, on an island.*) When does this story happen? (Call on a child. Ideas: *Over one year, in 1855, a long time ago.*)

Story Problem

The beginning of a story often has a problem that changes the everyday life of at least one of the characters. What problem did Birdie have in the story? (**Call on a child. Ideas:** *She didn't like living in the lighthouse. She was worried about her father because he was sick. She was worried about her brother who was at sea during a storm.*)

In stories with a problem, the problem changes the feelings of the characters, so they decide to do something about the problem. How did Birdie feel about her problem? (Call on a child. Ideas: *Worried, sad, lonely.*)

The middle of a story tells what the character does to try to solve a problem. This is called the attempt at solution. What did Birdie decide to do about her problem? (**Call on a child. Idea:** *She learned how to work the lighthouse so she could help her father.*)

The end of the story tells what happened that finally solved the problem. What was the solution to Birdie's problem? (**Call on a child. Ideas:** *Birdie kept the flame in the lighthouse burning through the storm. Her brother made it home safely. Her father got better.*)

Historical Fiction

(Show the Author's Note page from the end of the book to the children.) Sometimes authors add notes to their stories to tell us more information. Why do authors add notes to their stories? (Signal.) *To tell us more information.* (Read the Author's Note to the children.)

Stories that are about real people and things that really happened are called **nonfiction.** What are stories that are about real people and things that really happened called? (Signal.) *Nonfiction.* Stories that are about imaginary people and things are called **fiction.** What are stories about imaginary things and people called? (Signal.) *Fiction.* Is the story *Birdie's Lighthouse* about a real girl named Birdie living in a lighthouse on a real island named Turtle Island? (Signal.) *No.* So, this story is fiction. What kind of story is this? (Signal.) *Fiction.*

Birdie's Lighthouse is a special kind of fiction story. It is true that there was no Birdie and no Turtle Island. But, does the author tell us that there were real girls like Birdie living in lighthouses during this time? (Signal.) *Yes.* Does the author tell us that there were real lighthouses on islands like the one in the story on Turtle Island? (Signal.) *Yes.* This kind of fiction story is called **historical fiction.** What is this kind of fiction story called? (Signal.) *Historical fiction.*

Illustrations

Let's look at the illustrations that Kimberly Bulcken Root made. There are many different ways to make illustrations for a book: you can paint them; you can draw them with a pen or pencil; you can make them with markers, crayons, or chalk. How do you think Kimberly Bulcken Root made her illustrations? (**Call on a child. Idea:** *Watercolors and pencil.*)

Recalling Information

Let's remember some of the things we learned about *Birdie's Lighthouse*, and I'll write them down for you.

Note: Use the cumulative wall chart started in Lesson 1 for recording information from the "Recalling Information" activity in this literature lesson.

What is the title of today's book? (Signal.) Birdie's Lighthouse. (Write the title on the chart.)

Who are the important characters in this story? (Call on different children. Ideas: *Birdie, Mama, Papa, Nate, Janey.* Record on chart.)

Tell me a word that describes each character. (Call on different children. Accept two words for each character. Record on chart.)

Where does this story take place? (Call on a child. Ideas: *In a lighthouse, on an island, by the sea.* Record on chart.)

When does this story take place? (Call on a child. Idea: *In 1855. Over one year, a long time ago.* Record on chart.)

What was Birdie's problem in the story? (Call on a child. Ideas: *She didn't like living in the lighthouse. She was worried about her sick father. She was worried about her brother who was at sea during a storm.* Record on chart.)

How did that problem make Birdie feel? (Call on a child. Ideas: *Worried, upset, lonely.* Record on chart.)

How did Birdie attempt to solve her problem? (Call on a child. Idea: *She learned how to look after the lighthouse.* Record on chart.)

What was the solution to Birdie's problem? (Call on a child. Ideas: *She kept the flame going in the lighthouse through the storm. Her brother made it home safely. Her father got better.* Record on chart.)

Activity

Writing/Presenting

Title: *Birdie's Diary*

Time Required: 15 minutes each day for five days
Materials Required: Notebook or paper for writing

Procedure

1. Raise your hand if you can tell us who the most important character is in the story *Birdie's Lighthouse.* (Call on a child. *Birdie.*) Raise your hand if you can tell us who is telling about the things that happen in the story. (Call on a child. *Birdie.*) Another way to say that Birdie is the one telling about the things that happen in this story is to say that this story is told from Birdie's point of view. Raise your hand if you can tell us another way to say that Birdie is the one telling about the things that happened in the story. (Call on a child. *The story is told from Birdie's point of view.*) This means that we see the things that happen in the story through Birdie's eyes.

2. This book is special because it is written like a diary. (Show the children a few pages and point to the dates that are written before each diary entry.) A diary is a book where you write about things you do and how you feel. What is a diary? (Signal.) *A book where you write about things you do and how you feel.*

3. (Read the last sentence of the entry for September 11 and the second paragraph of the entry for November 30 to the children.) A logbook is a little bit like a diary because you can write in it every day. A logbook is different from a diary because you write in it about only one kind of thing. Why is a logbook different from a diary? (Signal.) *Because you write in it only about one kind of thing.* Another thing that is different about a logbook is that everybody can write in the same one. What is another thing that is different about a logbook? (Signal.) *Everybody can write in the same one.* Do different people write about what they do and how they feel in the same diary? (Signal.) *No.* Raise your hand if you can tell us what kind of thing Birdie and her father wrote about in the logbook. (Call on a child. Ideas: *Things that happen in the lighthouse, the sea, the weather.*) Raise your hand if you can tell us some of the things that Birdie wrote about in her diary. (Call on several children. Accept any reasonable response.)

4. (Read the first paragraph of the last page of the story to the children.) Raise your hand if you can tell us on what date Birdie finished writing in her old diary? (Call on a child. Idea: *January 15, 1856.* Write this date on the chalkboard for the children to refer to when you talk about writing in their diaries.) What did Papa promise to bring Birdie from the village? (Signal.) *A new diary.*

5. Today you are going to pretend that you are Birdie and it is January 16, 1856. Who are you going to pretend to be? (Signal.) *Birdie.* When are you going to pretend it is? (Signal.) *January 16, 1856.* Papa just got back from the village with a brand-new diary.

6. (Hand out a notebook or paper to each child.) The diary in the story was for one year. This is a diary for one week. How long is this a diary for? (Signal.) *One week.* You are going to imagine that you are Birdie, and you will write in this diary from her point of view about the week after the story ended. What are you going to write about in the diary? (Signal.) *The week after the story ended.*

7. Raise your hand if you can tell us what the date would be the day after the story ended. (Call on a child.) *January 16, 1856.* (Write this date on the chalkboard.) Write this date at the top of the first page of your diary. Be sure to put a comma between the number of the day and the year. (Check.)

8. Let's think about some of the things that Birdie might write about in her diary. Raise your hand if you can tell us something that happened at the end of the story. (Call on two or three children. Ideas: *The brother made it home safely. The father got better. Birdie got a new kitten.*) Raise your hand if you have any ideas of how these things would change what Birdie does each day. (Call on several children. Accept any reasonable response. Ideas: *She would play with her new kitten. She would not*

have to work so hard because her father is not sick anymore. She would not be worried about her brother.)

9. Let's think about some kinds of things that Birdie would not write about. Is it summertime? (Signal.) *No.* Would Birdie write about going swimming in the sunshine? (Signal.) *No.* Did people have TVs in 1856? (Signal.) *No.* Would Birdie write about watching TV? (Signal.) *No.*

10. Raise your hand if you can tell us something that Birdie might write about. (Call on several children. Accept any reasonable response.) Now you're ready to write your own diaries from Birdie's point of view. When you're finished, pick your favorite entry. (Have children repeat this activity for five days, writing a different entry for each day. You may need to set the scene before each day of writing based on what the children wrote the previous day. Children may share their entries with classmates, a small group, or a partner.)

Technology

(Children may use a word processing program to record their journal entries on the computer.)

ADDITIONAL LITERATURE

Following are some additional titles that your students may enjoy during and following this lesson.

My Nine Lives by Clio by Marjorie Priceman

Amelia's Notebook by Marissa Moss

Castle Diary: The Journal of Tobias Burgess, Page transcribed by Richard Platt

Lesson 6

Language Skill Development

> **Skills:** Proofreading for correct use of quotation marks
> **Time Required:** 15 minutes

When characters in a story talk out loud, it is called dialogue. What is it called when the characters in a story talk out loud? (Signal.) *Dialogue.* When authors write stories they use punctuation marks called quotation marks to show that someone is talking. What do we call the punctuation marks that authors use to show that someone is talking? (Signal.) *Quotation marks.*

(Write a sentence on the chalkboard. **The deer said, I think that it will rain.** Touch under each word of the sentence as the children read aloud.) Read the sentence. (Signal.) *The deer said, I think that it will rain.* What did the deer say? (Signal.) *I think that it will rain.*

Quotation marks that are put before what the character says look like sixes. (Draw a set of opening quotation marks before the word I.) Quotation marks that are put at the end of what the character says look like nines. (Draw a set of closing quotation marks on the chalkboard after the period.)

(Repeat process for these sentences: **Come here! Sit! shouted the man at his dog. Sandy counted, One, two three.**)

When you are writing stories and paragraphs of your own, remember to proofread your writing for the correct use of quotation marks.

Literature

Dear Annie

by Judith Caseley

Prereading

Examining the Book

This is the book that I am going to share with you today. The title of this book is *Dear Annie*. What's the title of today's book? (Signal.) Dear Annie.

The author of this story is Judith Caseley. Who is the author of *Dear Annie*? (Signal.) *Judith Caseley.*

Sometimes the same person writes the story and makes the pictures. Sometimes the author and illustrator are two different people. Judith Caseley wrote this story and she made the pictures. Did the same person write the story and make the pictures for *Dear Annie*? (Signal.) *Yes.* Judith Caseley is both the author and the illustrator of this book. Who is the author of *Dear Annie*? (Signal.) *Judith Caseley.* Who is the illustrator of *Dear Annie*? (Signal.) *Judith Caseley.*

Making Predictions

(Assign each child a partner. Show children the front and back covers of the book.) Look at the front and back covers. Tell your partner what you think the story will be about. (Allow about one minute for sharing predictions.)

Raise your hand if you would like to tell us your prediction of what you think the story will be about. (Call on three different children. Accept reasonable responses.)

Reading the Story

I'm going to read the story aloud to you and show you the pictures. After I read the story to you, we will talk about the story. (Read the story with minimal interruptions.)

Discussing the Book

Story Pattern

Most books have a pattern. Let's see if we can figure out the pattern for this book. You tell me what happened in the story and I'll write it on the chalkboard.

> **Note:** As the children retell the story, make a story map of the main story events on the chalkboard similar to the sample in Lesson 2.

(Discuss the sequence of story events briefly to construct the story map.)

(Point to the story map that is on the chalkboard.) Look at the shape of this story. What do we call a story that starts and ends in different places? (Signal.) *A linear story.*

Characters and Setting

All stories have a beginning, a middle, and an ending. The beginning of a story tells about the characters that are in the story. What does the beginning of a story tell about? (Signal.) *The characters that are in the story.* Who are the most important characters in *Dear Annie*? (Call on different children. Ideas: *Annie, Grandfather, Mama.*)

The beginning also tells about the setting of the story. Raise your hand if you can tell me some of the places in *Dear Annie.* (Call on two or three children. Ideas: *Annie's house, Grandfather's house, school.*)

Now let's talk about when the story *Dear Annie* happens. (Show the children the first pair of pages in the story. Point to the picture of Annie in her crib.) Raise your hand if you can tell me how old Annie looks in this picture. (Call on a child. Ideas: *She's a baby, just born.*)

(Show the children the last page of the story.) Is Annie still a baby at the end of the story? (Signal.) *No.* Raise your hand if you can guess how old Annie is in this picture. (Call on two or three children. Accept reasonable responses.) Is *Dear Annie* a story about one day? (Signal.) *No.* Is *Dear Annie* a story about one year? (Signal.) *No.* The story *Dear Annie* happens over a long time. When does *Dear Annie* happen? (Signal.) *Over a long time.*

Illustrations

Let's look at the illustrations that Judith Caseley made. There are many different ways to make illustrations for a book: you can paint them; you can draw them with a pen or pencil; you can make them with markers, crayons, or chalk. How do you think Judith Caseley made her illustrations? (Call on a child. Idea: *Watercolors and markers.*)

Recalling Information

Let's remember some of the things we learned about *Dear Annie,* and I'll write them down for you.

What is the title of today's book? (Signal.) Dear Annie. (Write the title on the chart.)

Who are the important characters in this story? (Call on different children. Ideas: *Annie, Grandfather, Mama.* Record on chart.)

Tell me a word that describes each character. (Call on different children. Accept two words for each character. Record on chart.)

Where does this story take place? (Call on a child. Ideas: *Annie's house, Grandfather's house, school.* Record on chart.)

When does this story take place? (Call on a child. Ideas: *Over a long time, during Annie's lifetime.* Record on chart.)

Did Annie have a problem in the story? (Signal.) *No.* So we will leave this part of the chart blank.

Activity

Letter Writing/Drafting/Proofreading/Writing a Final Copy

Title: *Writing a Friendly Letter*

    Time Required: 60 minutes

    Preparation: Prepare a chart or an overhead with lines that show the format for writing a letter, as shown in BLM 6.

        Make sure that every child knows the zip code for his or her address.

        Assign each child an older child in the school who will be his or her pen pal.

    Materials Required: BLM 6, one copy for each child

        Camera, film

        Class chart titled "Proofreading Marks"

Procedure

1. Today you will learn to write a friendly letter. What will you learn to do? (Signal.) *Write a friendly letter.*

2. (Point to the chart or overhead.) This form shows the pattern for writing a friendly letter. (Point to the street address line.) I write my street address on this line. (Write a street address.) I make sure that I write capital letters for the name of my street. Where do I put capital letters? (Signal.) *On the name of your street.*

3. (Point to the city, state, and zip code line.) I write my city, state, and zip code on this line. (Write a city, state, and zip code.) I make sure that I write capital letters for the names of my city and my state. Where do I put capital letters? (Signal.) *On the*

names of your city and state. (Point to zip code.) This number is called a zip code. What's this number called? (Signal.) *A zip code.* The zip code tells the mail carrier where to deliver the letter. What does the zip code tell? (Signal.) *Where to deliver the letter.* (Point to the comma.) I make sure to put a comma between the city and the state. What do I put between the city and the state? (Signal.) *A comma.*

4. (Point to the date line.) I write the date on this line. (Write the date.) I make sure that I write a capital letter for the month. Where do I put a capital letter? (Signal.) *On the month.* I put a comma between the number of the day and the year. Where do I put a comma? (Signal.) *Between the number of the day and the year.*

5. (Point to the greeting line.) I write the greeting on this line. (Write the greeting.) I make sure that I write a capital letter for the word **dear** and for the person's name. Where do I write capital letters? (Signal.) *On the word dear and for the person's name.* (Point to the colon.) This mark is called a **colon.** What's this mark called? (Signal.) *A colon.* I make sure that I put a colon at the end of my greeting. What do I put at the end of my greeting? (Signal.) *A colon.*

6. (Point to the body of the letter.) What we write about is called the **body** of the letter. What do we call what we write about? (Signal.) *The body of the letter.* Before I start the first line of my letter, I indent. What do I do to the first line of my letter? (Signal.) *Indent.* Then I write the body of my letter. (Write a short note to another teacher in the school.)

7. (Point to the closing of the letter.) I write the closing on this line. (Write the closing.) The first word of the closing needs a capital. What does the first word of the closing need? (Signal.) *A capital.*

8. (Point to the signature line.) This is where I sign my name. What is the last thing I write? (Signal.) Your name.

9. (Give children BLM 6.) Today you will write a friendly letter to your school pen pal. A pen pal is a special friend to whom you write letters. What's a pen pal? (Signal.) *A special friend to whom you write letters.*

10. (Explain to the children that each of them has been assigned an older student in the school as a pen pal. Have children follow the model that you have prepared as they write drafts of their letters. Encourage children to tell about themselves and what they like to do in their letters. Have children ask their pen pals questions about things they would like to know.)

11. (Have children proofread letters with assistance using the proofreading marks. You will need to add the mark for **needs to indent ¶** and for **the word is spelled incorrectly** (thay.) Children may use a dictionary to help them find the correct spellings of words.)

12. (Ask children to prepare good copies of their letters. While children are working on their letters, take a photograph of each child for the child to include with his/her final draft.)

13. (Optional: You may wish to have the children address a legal-sized envelope to their pen pal.)

Technology

(Letters may be word-processed. Many word processing programs include a template for letter writing. Each child should have the opportunity to send and receive an e-mail message from his or her school pen pal.)

(Children may also use the Internet to participate in being a pen pal with a child from another school or from a pen pal service. If the children use the Internet pen pal services, make sure that it is a safe venue.)

ADDITIONAL LITERATURE

Following are some additional titles that your students may enjoy during and following this lesson.

My Brother, Ant by Betsy Byers

The Jolly Postman: Or Other People's Letters by Janet Ahlberg

_____

_____

_____

_____

_____

_____

_____

_____

_____

_____

_____

_____

_____

_____

_____

Lesson 7

Language Skill Development

Parts of Speech: Articles, Nouns, Verbs; Writing Simple Sentences

Time Required: 30 minutes
Preparation: Make three class charts: one titled "Articles," one titled "Nouns," one titled "Verbs."

Note: Words should be added to the charts listed above at the beginning of each language skill development lesson for lessons 7–12.

What we say is called **speech.** What do we call what we say? (Signal.) *Speech.* Words are called the **parts of speech.** What are words called? (Signal.) *The parts of speech.*

Words used for persons, animals, places, or things are called **nouns.** What do we call words used for persons, animals, places, or things? (Signal.) *Nouns.*

(Point to the chart titled "Nouns.") The title of this chart is **Nouns.** My turn to write a noun that is a person. Ann. (Write Ann on chart.) Raise your hand if you can tell us a noun that is a person. (Call on three different children. Ideas: *Bob, man, girl.* Record each child's response on the chart. Repeat process for animals, places, and things.)

Doing words are called **verbs.** What do we call doing words? (Signal.) *Verbs.*

(Point to the chart titled "Verbs.") The title of this chart is **Verbs.** My turn to write a verb. (Write three verbs on the chart.) Raise your hand if you can tell us a word that is a verb. (Call on several different children. Ideas: *Running, eats, made.* Record each child's response on the chart.)

The words **an, a,** and **the** are called articles. What do we call the words **an, a,** and **the**? (Signal.) *Articles.*

(Point to the chart titled "Articles.") The title of this chart is **Articles.** There are only three words that are called articles. What are the three articles? (Signal.) *An, a, and the.* (Write the three articles on the chart.)

Knowing about parts of speech can help us write better sentences. If I put an article (write **A** on chalkboard) plus a noun (write **+ N** on the chalkboard) plus a verb (write **+ V** on the chalkboard), I have a simple sentence. My turn to write a simple sentence. (Write under the sentence pattern: The fox ran.) Read my sentence. (Signal.) *The fox ran.* (Repeat process for: **A boss walked. An egg rolled.**)

(Have children write simple sentences of their own using the A+N+V pattern on paper or in a notebook. Encourage children to write the sounds they hear in words and to use charts and dictionaries as sources for correct spelling. Children should be expected to correctly spell words taught in formal lessons. Have children skip a line between sentences. Ask three or four children to read their sentences aloud to the class or to read their sentences to a partner. Keep these copies of the children's sentences for the next lesson.)

Literature

Jeremiah Learns to Read

by Jo Ellen Bogart

Illustrated by Laura Fernandez and Rick Jacobson

Prereading

Examining the Book

This is the next book that I am going to share with you. The title of this book is *Jeremiah Learns to Read.* What's the title of today's book? (Signal.) Jeremiah Learns to Read.

The author of this story is Jo Ellen Bogart. Who is the author of *Jeremiah Learns to Read*? (Signal.) *Jo Ellen Bogart.*

Some books have more than one illustrator. Sometimes, people help each other make a book. This book has two illustrators. The illustrators of this book are Laura Fernandez and Rick Jacobson. Who are the illustrators of *Jeremiah Learns to Read*? (Signal.) *Laura Fernandez and Rick Jacobson.*

Making Predictions

(Show the children the front and back covers of the book.) Look at the front and back covers. Raise your hand if you can ask a **who** question that will help us make predictions about this story. (Call on a child. Ideas: *Who is the old man? Who is reading the book? Who is with him?*) Raise your hand if you can ask a **what** question that will help us make predictions about this story. (Call on a child. Ideas: *What is the old man doing on the front cover? What is he doing on the back cover? What is the old man holding on the front cover? What are the children doing?*) Raise your hand if you can ask a **where** question that will help us make predictions about this story. (Call on a child. Ideas: *Where is everyone? Where does the story take place?*)

Reading the Story

I'm going to read the story aloud to you and show you the pictures. After I read the story to you, we will talk about the story. (Read the story with minimal interruptions.)

Discussing the Book

Story Pattern

Most books have a pattern. Let's see if we can figure out the pattern for this book. You tell me what happened in the story and I'll write it on the chalkboard.

> **Note:** As the children retell the story, make a story map of the main story events on the chalkboard similar to the sample in Lesson 2.

(Discuss the sequence of story events briefly to construct the story map.)

(Point to the story map that is on the chalkboard.) Look at the shape of this story. (Show the children the first page of the story.) Does this part of the story tell us when the story happens? (Signal.) *Yes.* Yes, the illustration shows us it is day. (Flip through the next three pages.) The next few pages tell us about Jeremiah. Do they show when the story takes place? (Signal.) *Yes.* Yes, the illustrations show us it is day because the sky is light blue. (Turn the page to where Jeremiah is talking to his wife.) How about now? Can we tell when the story takes place? (Signal.) *Yes.* Yes, the illustration shows us it is now night. The next picture is also dark. (Turn to the page where Jeremiah is combing his beard. Read the page.) Raise your hand if you can tell us how we know when the story takes place. (Call on different children. Ideas: *It starts with the next morning. He got dressed. He made breakfast. He packed lunch.*)

(Turn to a few more pages throughout the rest of the story.) Raise your hand if you can tell us what happens next. (Call on different children. Ideas: *Jeremiah goes to school. He learns to read and write. He teaches others how to do things. He reads to his wife.*) The pattern for this story is a linear story. What's the pattern for this story? (Signal.) *A linear story.*

Characters and Setting

All stories have a beginning, a middle, and an ending. The beginning of a story tells about the characters that are in the story. What does the beginning of a story tell about? (Signal.) *The characters that are in the story.* Who are the important characters in *Jeremiah Learns to Read*? (Call on different children. Ideas: *Jeremiah, Juliana/his wife, Mrs. Trumble/the teacher, the children.*)

The beginning also tells about the setting of the story. Where does this story happen? (Call on a child. Ideas: *In the country, on a farm, at school.*) Look at this picture. (Show children the picture where Jeremiah is teaching how to make applesauce.) What are the characters peeling? (Signal.) *Apples.* Apples grow in the fall. This illustration helps to tell us when the story takes place. Raise your hand if you can tell us when this story takes place. (Call on a child. Ideas: *In the past, in the fall.*)

Story Problem

The beginning of a story often has a problem that changes the everyday life of at least one of the characters. What problem did Jeremiah have in the story? (Call on a child. Ideas: *He couldn't read. He couldn't write.*)

In stories with a problem, the problem changes the feelings of the characters, so they decide to do something about the problem. How do you think Jeremiah felt about his problem? (Call on a child. Ideas: *Worried, sad, frustrated.*)

The middle of a story tells what the character does to try to solve a problem. This is called the attempt at solution. What did Jeremiah decide to do about his problem? (Call on a child. Idea: *He went to school.*)

The end of the story tells what happened that finally solved the problem. What was the solution to Jeremiah's problem? (Call on a child. Idea: *He learned to read.*)

Illustrations

Let's look at the illustrations that Laura Fernandez and Rick Jacobson made. There are many different ways to make illustrations for a book: you can paint them; you can draw them with a pen or pencil; you can make them with markers, crayons, or chalk. How do you think Laura Fernandez and Rick Jacobson made their illustrations? (Call on a child. Idea: *Oil on canvas.*)

Recalling Information

Let's remember some of the things we learned about *Jeremiah Learns to Read,* and I'll write them down for you.

Note: Use the cumulative wall chart started in Lesson 1 for recording information from the "Recalling Information" activity in this literature lesson.

What is the title of today's book? (Signal.) Jeremiah Learns to Read. (Write the title on the chart.)

Who are the important characters in this story? (Call on different children. Ideas: *Jeremiah, Juliana/his wife, Mrs. Trumble/the teacher, the children.* Record on chart.)

Tell me a word that describes each character. (Call on different children. Accept two words for each character. Record on chart.)

Where does this story take place? (Call on a child. Ideas: *In the country, on a farm, at school.* Record on chart.)

When does this story take place? (Call on a child. Ideas: *In the fall, in the past.* Record on chart.)

What was Jeremiah's problem in the story? (Call on a child. Idea: *He couldn't read.* Record on chart.)

How did that problem make Jeremiah feel? (Call on a child. Ideas: *Worried, sad, frustrated.* Record on chart.)

How did Jeremiah attempt to solve his problem? (Call on a child. Idea: *He went to school.* Record on chart.)

What was the solution to Jeremiah's problem? (Call on a child. Idea: *He learned to read.* Record on chart.)

Activity

Listening for feeling or mood in a musical or written selection/Expressing feeling or mood with face and/or body posture/Reading poetry chorally

Title: *Mood Swings*

Time Required: 40 minutes

Materials Required: Music selections representing happy or somber moods as suggested in the following chart (or choose suitable instrumental music at your own discretion)

A compact disc and/or tape player

Two pieces of chart paper and chart pens in two colors

BLM 7A, one copy for each child (the poem *Things that Go "Bump!" in the Night!* by Rick Williams)

Mood Music

Suggested instrumental music evocative of a happy mood	Suggested instrumental music evocative of a somber mood
Tchaikovsky "Miniature Overture" "Trepak: Russian Dance" "Dance of the Mirlitons" from *The Nutcracker*	**Mozart** Symphony No. 40 in G minor, first movement
Johann Strauss "Schneeglocken Walzer" ("Snowdrop Waltz") "An der Schonen Blauen Donau" ("Blue Danube Waltz")	**Chopin** Prelude in E minor
Johann Strauss "Tritsch-Tratsch-Polka" "Chit-Chat Polka"	**Grieg** "Ase's Death" and "Morning" from *Peer Gynt Suite*

Procedure

1. (Choose one piece of music that sounds bright and happy and one piece of music that sounds dark and somber.) Today we are going to listen to two pieces of music. The first piece is by (composer's name) and the second is by (composer's name). Both pieces are instrumental music. What kind of music are they? (Signal.) *Instrumental music.* Instrumental music has no words, only instruments. What does instrumental music have? (Signal.) *No words, only instruments.*

2. Listening to music is a special skill that needs to be practiced to be learned. The best way to listen carefully is to sit up straight, fold our hands neatly in front of us, and close our eyes. Show me what you will look like when you are ready to listen carefully. (Check for children to be sitting up straight with folded hands and closed eyes. Do not begin the listening activity until all are showing appropriate listening behavior.)

3. Listen carefully to the first piece of music. When the music ends, I will ask you to raise your hands and tell me how the music made you feel. (Play the first selection. If necessary, correct students' behavior by stopping the music, correcting the behavior, then starting the music again from the beginning.)

4. (When the selection ends, compliment children whose behavior has been appropriate.) Open your eyes and tell me how the music made you feel. (Chart several student responses on the first piece of chart paper. Ideas: *Happy, warm, bright, cheerful.*)

5. Let's listen to the second piece of music now. As you listen, remember to think about how the music makes you feel. Show me appropriate listening behavior. (Check to see that the behavior is appropriate before you begin the selection. Follow the corrective procedure outlined above as necessary.)

6. (When the selection ends, compliment children as outlined above.) Open your eyes and tell me how the music made you feel. (Chart several student responses on the second piece of chart paper. Ideas: *Sad, unhappy, dark, somber.*)

7. Composers know how to write music that inspires different feelings in us. You have made a good comparison between (the title of piece number 1) and (the title of piece number 2). You suggested that the first piece inspired a happy feeling or mood and that the second piece inspired a sad feeling or mood.

8. Authors and poets know how to write words that inspire different feelings in us. I am going to read you a poem today that changes from one feeling or mood to another. As I read, listen to see if you can hear what feelings the poet wanted to make you feel.

9. (Practice reading the poem before presenting it to the class. Then read *Things that Go "Bump!" in the Night!* from BLM 7A aloud to the class. In a quiet, mysterious, and somewhat ominous voice, read the first section of the poem, until the end of "Why is it night-noises always are vicious?" Take care to voice words like screechings and squawkings, whistles and clatters, tippings and tappings in a dramatic way—the point is to bring the sounds to life. Also use dark facial expressions to emphasize the darkness of the poetry. When you reach "Why can't they be something fun or delicious?" your delivery of the poem should become dramatically lighter and more cheerful. Use a brighter and happier-sounding voice. A gradually spreading smile on your face will help children to recognize that the frightening nighttime sounds are being transformed into pleasing nighttime sounds.)

10. Did the mood change in *Things that Go "Bump!" in the Night*? (Signal.) *Yes.* Tell about the way you felt when the poem started. (Call on several children. Ideas: *Scared, frightened, on edge.*) Tell about the way you felt when the poem ended. (Call on several children. Ideas: *Happier, not so scared, less frightened.*)

11. We can also show feelings or moods just by the expressions on our faces or by the way we hold our bodies. When I say **Go,** show me an expression with your face that tells me you are happy. Go! (Watch faces, choose good examples, and have students share with the class.) Now show me an expression with your face that tells me you are sad. Go! (Repeat above procedure to show body posture when happy, sad, angry, disappointed, and others at your discretion.)

12. (Divide the children into groups. Assign children parts of the poem to practice reading aloud chorally. Everyone may join in for the repeating parts of the poem.)

Listening/Choral Reading/Descriptive Words/Poetry Writing

Title: *A Found Poem*

Time Required: 40–50 minutes

Materials Required: A descriptive passage of your choice or the descriptive passage on BLM 7B, one copy for each student

A found poem of your own, or the one provided, generated from the teaching passage printed onto chart paper

A piece of chart paper headed "Describing Words"; chart pens

Two pieces of 8.5" x 11" lined paper for each student; one piece of 8.5" x 11" blank paper for each child; pencils, erasers, and pencil crayons or crayons for each child

Procedure

1. (Read the descriptive passage from BLM 7B aloud to the children with no introduction.) The passage I have just read to you contains many describing words. I will read it again. When I am finished, raise your hand to tell me the describing words you heard in the passage. (Read the passage again.)

2. Tell me about the describing words you heard in this passage. (Call on several children. Chart the responses on the chart paper.)

3. (Give a copy of the passage to each child.) This time, we will read together. Let's see if we can add some descriptive words to our chart. (Read again and chart additional descriptive words.)

4. Your task today is to create a found poem. What kind of poem are you going to write? (Signal.) *A found poem.* A **found poem** is a poem made of words that you find in a descriptive passage like the one you have just read. Where do you find the words for a found poem? (Signal.) *In a descriptive passage.* You choose the words with sounds you like from the passage. Then you put them together in an order that you like. Your poem does not need to rhyme. Does your poem need to rhyme? (Signal.) *No.* All it needs are words from the passage with sounds you like, put into an order that you like.

5. Here is a found poem that I wrote using the words from the passage we read together. I like the sounds of these words and I like the order in which I put them. (Read the poem to the class. Then have the class read the poem with you.)

Duck

Rain

Wind

Whoosh!

Feet

Swishing

Slapping

Whack! Whack!

Duck

6. You may use the words you choose in any order. You may repeat them if you wish. While you are planning your poem, you may make a list of words with sounds you like on the draft sheet I gave you. Then put them in the order that sounds good to you. When you have finished your draft copy, bring it to me before making your good copy. If you have finished your draft copy and I am busy with another student, take a piece of blank paper and make an illustration to go with your found poem.

7. (Assess and proof draft copies as they arrive. Since the words are all included in the descriptive passage, children should be expected to spell the words correctly. When the poems and illustrations are completed, post them in the classroom. Set aside 10–15 minutes for a "Gallery Walk" so that children can read their classmates' poems and view their illustrations.)

ADDITIONAL LITERATURE

Following are some additional titles that your students may enjoy during and following this lesson.

The Wednesday Surprise by Eve Bunting

Read for Me, Mama by Vashanti Rahaman

Things that Go "Bump!" in the Night!

Just around bed-time, as you may recall,
things start to scuttle inside of your walls!
Pieces of puzzles, an old rubber boot,
which in the daylight seemed quiet and mute—

things that fall over and "whump!" just for spite—
these are the things that go "bump!" in the night!

Screechings and squawkings and groanings and gripes
might be related to your water pipes.
Tippings and tappings and drummings and dingles
Originate with the rain on the shingles—

things that you don't hear at all in the light—
these are the things that go "bump!" in the night!

Whistles and clatters of wind in the willows
aren't blocked out when a head's under pillows.
Howlings of sirens like wolves in their lairs
will not be silenced by your "I'm not scared!"s.

Things that stay just beyond your line of sight—
these are the things that go "bump!" in the night!

Who was it told us, what cruel visionary,
decided that night-time should always be scary?
Why is it night-noises always are vicious?
Why can't they be something fun or delicious?

So. . .

Tonight when you climb to the top of the stairs,
snuggle in blankets and whisper your prayers,
remember how rain when it's falling on shingles,
sounds pretty much just like chocolate sprinkles,
showering down gently to your great delight

and forget about things that go "bump!" in the night!

Original poetry by Rick Williams, 2001

A descriptive passage for use with the second activity in Lesson 7.

It was raining. It wasn't raining a minute ago, but it was raining now. It was raining hard. When the wind was gentle, the rain poured straight down on Dilly Duck. When the wind was strong, the rain blew "Whoosh!" straight into Dilly Duck's face. Rain dripped from Dilly Duck's bill, drip, drip, drip, drop, drip, drip, drip, drop. Dilly Duck didn't mind. He liked the rain. His oily feathers shed the water and kept his body warm and dry. Dilly Duck splashed in the puddles on his way to the pond. His webbed feet made a soft swishing sound on the grass. They made a slapping sound in the mud on the shore. Then with a happy "Whack, whack, whack!" Dilly Duck slipped into the pond. In the water, his strong webbed feet made no sound at all. All around him, raindrops dimpled the pond. But the water was calm and safe between the reeds. Dilly Duck was home.

Write the draft for your found poem on a sheet of lined paper.

Lesson 8

Language Skill Development

Parts of speech: articles, nouns, verbs, adjectives; editing sentences using a caret; writing simple sentences

Time Required: 30 minutes

Preparation: Make a class chart titled "Adjectives."
Write these sentences on the chalkboard: The fox ran.
A boss walked. An egg rolled.

Materials Required: Class charts from Lesson 7
Children's sentences written in Lesson 7 (Each child should have a copy of his or her own work.)

What we say is called speech. What do we call what we say? (Signal.) *Speech.* Words are called the parts of speech. What are words called? (Signal.) *The parts of speech.*

What do we call words used for persons, animals, places, or things? (Signal.) *Nouns.*

(Point to the "Nouns" chart.) Raise your hand if you have any words that are nouns that you would like to add to our class chart. (Call on different children. Ideas: *Bev, dog, city, ball.*)

What do we call **doing** words? (Signal.) *Verbs.*

(Point to the "Verbs" chart.) Raise your hand if you have any words that are verbs that you would like to add to our class chart. (Call on different children. Ideas: *said, singing, plays.*)

What do we call the words **an, a,** and **the**? (Signal.) *Articles.* We don't need to add to the chart because there are only three articles.

Describing words are called **adjectives.** What do we call describing words? (Signal.) *Adjectives.*

(Point to the chart titled "Adjectives.") The title of this chart is **Adjectives.** My turn to write an adjective. (Write three adjectives on the chart.) Raise your hand if you can tell us a word that is an adjective. (Call on several different children. Ideas: *big, yellow, beautiful.* Record each child's response on the chart.)

Knowing about parts of speech can help us write better sentences. (Point to the sentences on the chalkboard.) These are the sentences that I wrote during the last lesson. I can make better sentences by adding an adjective to each of my sentences. (Demonstrate using a caret to add the word **sly** before **fox** in the first sentence.) I use this mark called a caret to show that I'm adding a word to my sentence. (Point.) What does this mark mean? (Signal.) *That I'm adding a word to my sentence.* (Repeat process for remaining sentences. Add **happy** before **boss** and **interesting** before **egg.**)

(Give each child his or her own copy of the sentences written during Lesson 7.) These are the simple sentences you wrote during the last lesson. Use a caret to add an adjective to each of your sentences. If you need help with a word, you may look on the class chart. (Ask three or four children to read their sentences aloud to the class or to read their sentences to a partner.)

If I put an article (write **A** on chalkboard) plus an adjective (write **+ Adj** on the chalkboard) plus a noun (write **+ N** on the chalkboard) plus a verb (write **+ V** on the chalkboard), I have a sentence that is harder than the one I wrote in the last lesson. My turn to write a new sentence. (Write under the sentence pattern: **The old man shouted.**) Read my sentence. (Signal.) *The old man shouted.*

(Have children write simple sentences of their own using the A+Adj+N+V pattern on paper or in a notebook. Encourage children to write the sounds they hear in words and to use charts and dictionaries as sources for correct spelling. Children should be expected to correctly spell words taught in formal lessons. Ask three or four children to read their sentences aloud to the class or to read their sentences to a partner. Keep these copies of the children's sentences for the next lesson.)

(Add caret proofreading mark to class chart titled "Proofreading Marks.")

Literature

John Henry

by Julius Lester

Illustrated by Jerry Pinkney

Prereading

Examining the Book

This is the book that I am going to share with you today. The title of this book is *John Henry.* What's the title of today's book? (Signal.) John Henry.

The author of this story is Julius Lester. Who is the author of *John Henry*? (Signal.) *Julius Lester.*

The illustrator of this book is Jerry Pinkney. Who is the illustrator of *John Henry*? (Signal.) *Jerry Pinkney.*

Story Genre/Figurative Language

There are many different kinds of stories. The story *John Henry* is a special kind of story called a legend. What kind of story is *John Henry*? (Signal.) *A legend.* A **legend** is a very old story. What's a legend? (Signal.) *A very old story.*

There are also different kinds of legends. *John Henry* is a special kind of legend called a folktale. What kind of legend is *John Henry*? *A folktale.* **Folktales** are stories that have been told by people for a long time. What are folktales? (Signal.) *Stories that have been told by people for a long time.* Folktales are often stories about things that happen in the country or in small towns. Do folktales usually tell stories about things that happened in the city? (Signal.) *No.* Do folktales usually tell about things that happened in the country or in small towns? (Signal.) *Yes.*

Legends and folktales often use exaggeration to make the story more fun. What do legends and folktales often use to make the story more fun? (Signal.) *Exaggeration.* **Exaggeration** is making something seem bigger, stronger, or better than it really is. What is exaggeration? (Signal.) *Making something seem bigger, stronger, or better than it really is.*

If I told you that my dog is as big as a dinosaur, would you believe me? (Signal.) *No.* A dog as big as a Tyrannosaurus rex is an exaggeration. What is a dog that is as big as a Tyrannosaurus rex? (Signal.) *An exaggeration.* If I told you that my dog is about as big as my pillow, would you believe me? (Signal.) *Yes.* Is a dog about the size of a pillow an exaggeration? (Signal.) *No.* If I told you that I am so strong that I could lift an airplane, would you believe me? (Signal.) *No.* Is this an exaggeration? (Signal.) *Yes.*

Stories that use a lot of exaggeration are called **tall tales.** What are stories that use a lot of exaggeration called? (Signal.) *Tall tales. John Henry* uses a lot of exaggeration, so it is also a tall tale. Why is *John Henry* also a tall tale? (Signal.) *It uses a lot of exaggeration.*

Raise your hand if you can remember one of the kinds of story that *John Henry* is. (Call on up to three children. Ideas: *Legend, folktale, tall tale.*)

Reading the Story

I'm going to read the story aloud to you and show you the pictures. After I read the story to you, we will talk about the story. (Read the story with minimal interruptions.)

Discussing the Book

Story Pattern

Most books have a pattern. Let's see if we can figure out the pattern for this book. You tell me what happened in the story and I'll write it on the chalkboard.

Note: As the children retell the story, make a story map of the main story events on the chalkboard similar to the sample in Lesson 2.

(Discuss the sequence of story events briefly to construct the story map.)

(Point to the story map that is on the chalkboard.) Look at the shape of this story. It's a line. What do we call a story that starts and ends in different places? (Signal.) *A linear story.*

Characters and Setting

All stories have a beginning, a middle, and an ending. The beginning of a story tells about the characters that are in the story. What does the beginning of a story tell about? (Signal.) *The characters that are in the story.* Who is the most important character in *John Henry*? (Signal.) *John Henry.*

The beginning also tells about the setting of the story. Raise your hand if you can tell us something about where the story *John Henry* happened. (Call on two or three children. Ideas: *On the road, on the railroad, in the South, in a mountain.*)

Now let's think about when the story *John Henry* happened. (Show the children the pair of pages where John Henry and Ferret-Faced Freddy have the race.) Look at the buildings in this picture. Do they look like buildings that you would see in a town today? (Signal.) *No.* Raise your hand if you can tell us when you think you would have seen buildings like these. (Call on a child. Idea: *A long time ago.*) This story happened a long time ago. When did the story *John Henry* happen? (Signal.) *A long time ago.*

> **Note:** You may want to read to the children some of the page at the beginning of the book that tells about the history of John Henry. If you do this, you can be more specific with the setting. It tells us that this legend stems from events that took place in 1870–1873 in West Virginia.

Story Problem

Stories often have a problem that changes the everyday life of at least one of the characters. Throughout the story John Henry has many different small problems instead of one big problem. What does John Henry have instead of one big problem? (Signal.) *Many different small problems.*

(Show the children the page where John Henry meets Ferret-Faced Freddy.) Raise your hand if you can remember what the problem is in this part of the story. (Call on a child. Idea: *Ferret-Faced Freddy was mean.* If the children are unable to recall this information, you can reread the page, then ask again.)

The part of a story that tells what the character does to try to solve a problem is called the attempt at solution. What did John Henry decide to do about his problem? (Call on a child. Ideas: *He made a bet with Freddy. Freddy and John Henry had a race, with Freddy on his horse and John Henry on his feet. If Freddy lost, he had to be nice for a year.*)

The part of the story that tells what happened that finally solved the problem is called the solution to the problem. What was the solution to John Henry's problem? (Call on a child. Ideas: *John Henry won the race. Ferret-Faced Freddy had to be nice. Ferret-Faced Freddy became Frederick the Friendly.*)

(Show and reread the page where John Henry meets the men working on the road.) What is the problem in this part of the story? (Call on a child. Idea: *There's a big boulder blocking the road.*) What did John Henry do to try to solve this problem? (Call on a child. Ideas: *He offered to lend the men a hand. He used his hammers to break up the boulder.*) What was the solution to John Henry's problem? (Call on a child. Ideas: *He broke apart the boulder. He cleared the way for the road.*)

(Show children the pair of pages with the picture of the mountain.) Raise your hand if you can remember the problem in this part of the story. (Call on a child. Idea: *They needed to make a tunnel through the mountain for the railroad.*) What did John Henry do to try to solve this problem? (Call on a child. Idea: *He used his hammer to break the rocks.*) What was the solution to John Henry's problem? (Call on a child. Ideas: *He made a tunnel in the mountain. He was faster than the drill.*)

Raise your hand if you can tell us which of John Henry's problems was the biggest. (Call on a child. Idea: *Making a tunnel in the mountain.*)

Parts of legends are thought to be true. Do you think that people believed that all the things in this story really happened? (Signal.) *No.* Do you think people might have believed that John Henry existed and was really strong? (Signal.) *Yes.*

Illustrations

(Point to the medal on the front cover.) This book is special because it won second prize for its pictures. This prize it won is called the Caldecott Medal. What prize did the book *John Henry* win? (Signal.) *The Caldecott Medal.* Raise your hand if you can tell us the name of another book we read that won this prize. (Call on a child. Ideas: A Chair for My Mother, Grandfather's Journey.)

Let's look at the illustrations that Jerry Pinkney made. There are many different ways to make illustrations for a book: you can paint them; you can draw them with a pen or pencil; you can make them with markers, crayons, or chalk. How do you think Jerry Pinkney made his illustrations? (Call on a child. Idea: *Watercolors and pencil.*)

Recalling Information

Let's remember some of the things we learned about *John Henry,* and I'll write them down for you.

Note: Use the cumulative wall chart started in Lesson 1 for recording information from the "Recalling Information" activity in this literature lesson.

What is the title of today's book? (Signal.) John Henry. (Write the title on the chart.)

Who is the most important character in this story? (Call on a child. Idea: *John Henry.* Record on chart.)

Tell me a word that describes this character. (Call on different children. Accept two words for the character. Record on chart.)

Where does this story take place? (Call on a child. Ideas: *On a road, on a railroad, in West Virginia.* Record on chart.)

When does this story take place? (Call on a child. Ideas: *A long time ago; 1870–1873.* Record on chart.)

What was John Henry's biggest problem in the story? (Call on a child. Idea: *He needed to make a tunnel through the mountain.* Record on chart.)

How did that problem make John Henry feel? (Call on a child. Ideas: *Determined, strong, tired.* Record on chart.)

How did John Henry attempt to solve his problem? (Call on a child. Idea: *He used his hammers.* Record on chart.)

What was the solution to John Henry's problem? (Call on a child. Idea: *He made a tunnel through the mountain. He worked faster than the drill.* Record on chart.)

Technology

Have children complete a search on the Internet for the songs about John Henry. Use the Google search engine with the key words **John Henry** (www.ibiblio.org/john_henry/resources1.html). Extensive bibliographies of printed, visual, and recorded John Henry materials are included. Songs may be heard from the Internet.

Reader Preference

(Have children listen to one of the songs about John Henry.) Think about which you liked best—the song or the storybook about John Henry.

Raise your hand if you liked the song the best. (Remind children that they can vote only once.) Tell me why you liked the song the best. (Call on different children. Accept one reason for each child. Repeat process for storybook.)

ADDITIONAL LITERATURE

Following are some additional titles that your students may enjoy during and following this lesson.

Swamp Angel by Anne Isaacs

The Talking Eggs by Robert D. San Souci

Pecos Bill by Steven Kellogg

Lesson 9

Language Skill Development

Parts of speech: articles, nouns, verbs, adjectives, adverbs; editing sentences using a caret; writing simple sentences

Time Required: 30 minutes

Preparation: Make a class chart titled "Adverbs."

Write these sentences on the chalkboard: The sly fox ran. A happy boss walked. An interesting egg rolled.

Materials Required: Class charts from lessons 7, 8

Children's sentences written in Lesson 8. (Each child should have a copy of his or her own work.)

What we say is called **speech.** What do we call what we say? (Signal.) *Speech.* Words are called the parts of speech. What are words called? (Signal.) *The parts of speech.*

What do we call words used for persons, animals, places, or things? (Signal.) *Nouns.* (Add nouns to class chart.)

What do we call **doing** words? (Signal.) *Verbs.* (Add verbs to class chart.)

What do we call the words **an, a,** and **the**? (Signal.) *Articles.* We don't need to add to the chart because there are only three articles.

What do we call **describing** words? (Signal.) *Adjectives.* (Add adjectives to class chart.)

Words that tell how and when are called **adverbs.** What do we call words that tell how and when? (Signal.) *Adverbs.*

(Point to the chart titled "Adverbs.") The title of this chart is **Adverbs.** My turn to write an adverb. (Write **fast, yesterday,** and **slowly** on the chart.) Raise your hand if you can tell us a word that is an adverb. (Call on several different children. Ideas: *Quietly, today, merrily.* Record each child's response on the chart.)

Knowing about parts of speech can help us write better sentences. (Point to the sentences on the chalkboard.) These are the sentences that I wrote during the last lesson. I can make better sentences by adding an adverb to each of my sentences. (Demonstrate using a caret to add **fast** to the end of the first sentence.) I use this mark called a caret to show that I'm adding a word to my sentence. (Point.) What does this mark mean? (Signal.) *That I'm adding a word to my sentence.* (Repeat process for remaining sentences. Add **yesterday** after **walked** and **quickly** after **rolled.**)

(Give each child his or her own copy of the sentences written during lessons 7 and 8.) Touch the sentences to which you added an adjective. (Check.) Use a caret to add an adverb to each of your sentences. If you need help with a word, you may look on the class chart. (Ask three or four children to read their sentences aloud to the class or to read their sentences to a partner.)

If I put an article (write **A** on chalkboard) plus an adjective (write **+ Adj** on the chalkboard) plus a noun (write **+ N** on the chalkboard) plus a verb (write **+ V** on the chalkboard) plus an adverb (write **+ Adv** on the chalkboard), I have a sentence that is harder than the one I wrote in the last lesson.

My turn to write a new sentence. (Write under the sentence pattern: The little kitten jumped high.) Read my sentence. (Signal.) *The little kitten jumped high.*

(Have children write simple sentences of their own using the A+Adj+N+V+Adv pattern on paper or in a notebook. Children should be expected to use capitals and periods correctly as taught in Lesson 5. Encourage children to write the sounds they hear in words and to use charts and dictionaries as sources for correct spelling. Children should be expected to spell words taught in formal lessons correctly. Ask three or four children to read their sentences aloud to the class or to read their sentences to a partner. Keep these copies of the children's sentences for the next lesson.)

Literature

Atalanta's Race: A Greek Myth

by Shirley Climo

Illustrated by Alexander Koshkin

Prereading

Examining the Book

This is the next book that I am going to share with you. The title of this book is *Atalanta's Race: A Greek Myth.* What's the title of today's book? (Signal.) Atalanta's Race: A Greek Myth.

Some stories are so old that the author is remembered only by his or her first or last name. Sometimes the author isn't known. The author of this story is unknown, but the author of this version of the story is Shirley Climo. In this book, she retells a very old story. Who is the author of this book? (Signal.) *Shirley Climo.*

The illustrator of this book is Alexander Koshkin. Who is the illustrator of *Atalanta's Race: A Greek Myth*? (Signal.) *Alexander Koshkin.*

Story Genre

Today's story is called a myth. **Myths** are very old stories about superhuman beings, like gods, heroes, and monsters. These stories sometimes try to explain how things in nature started, such as why the sun rises or why volcanoes erupt.

Day 1

Reading the Story

I'm going to read the first half of the story today. Tomorrow I'll read the second half. After I read the story to you, we will talk about the story. (**Read the story up to the first race, with minimal interruptions.**)

This story is set in Ancient Greece more than three thousand years ago. Listen as I read; there may be words and things that you don't understand. If you hear something that you do not understand, raise your hand and ask me a question about it. I will give you an answer that helps you understand. When you give people an answer that helps them understand, you are giving **clarification.** What are you doing when you give people an answer that helps them understand? (Signal.) *Giving clarification.*

Discussing the Story

Story Pattern

Most books have a pattern. Let's see if we can figure out the pattern for this book. You tell me what happened in the story so far, and I'll write it on the chalkboard.

Note: As the children retell the story, make a story map of the main story events on the chalkboard similar to the sample in Lesson 1.

(Briefly discuss the sequence of story events to construct the story map.)

(Point to the story map that is on the chalkboard.) Look at the shape of this story. It's a circle. This story starts and ends in the same place. What do we call a story that starts and ends in the same place? (Signal.) *A circle story.*

Characters and Setting

All stories have a beginning, a middle, and an ending. The beginning of a story tells about the characters that are in the story. What does the beginning of a story tell about? (Signal.) *The characters that are in the story.* Who are the important characters, so far, in *Atalanta's Race: A Greek Myth*? (Call on different children. Ideas: *Atalanta, King Iasus, Ciron.*)

The beginning also tells about the setting of the story. (Show children page 4.) Look at this picture. This illustration helps to tell us where and when the story takes place. The story and the pictures tell where this story takes place. Where does this story take place? (Call on a child. Ideas: *In a kingdom, on a mountain, in a palace.*) Raise your hand if you can tell us when this story takes place. (Call on a child. Ideas: *Long ago, in the past.*)

Illustrations

Let's look at the illustrations that Alexander Koshkin made. There are many different ways to make illustrations for a book: you can paint them; you can draw them with a pen or pencil; you can make them with markers, crayons, or chalk. How do you think Alexander Koshkin made his illustrations? (Call on a child. Idea: *With watercolors.*)

Day 2

Reading the Story

I'm going to read the second half of the story today. After I read the story to you, we will talk about the story. (Read the story with minimal interruptions.)

Discussing the Story

We already talked about the setting and some of the characters from the first half of the story. Are there any new settings? (Signal.) *Yes.* Raise your hand if you can tell us some new or old settings. (Call on different children. Ideas: *A field, down by the sea, the palace.*) Are there any new characters? (Signal.) *Yes.* Raise your hand if you can tell us one of them. (Call on different children. Ideas: *Melanion; Aphrodite, the goddess of love; Rhea, the mother goddess.*)

At first, Aphrodite helps Melanion win Atalanta's love; but at the end of the story, Aphrodite has them both turned into lions. Raise your hand if you can tell us why you think she would do that. (Call on different children. Ideas: *They didn't thank her. They cared only about hunting and games and races.*)

Note: You may wish to read the Author's Note at the end of the book to provide children with further information about the myth and the Olympics.

Recalling Information

Let's remember some of the things we learned about *Atalanta's Race: A Greek Myth,* and I'll write them down for you.

Note: Use the cumulative wall chart started in Lesson 1 for recording information from the "Recalling Information" activity in this literature lesson.

What is the title of today's book? (Signal.) Atalanta's Race: A Greek Myth. (Write the title on the chart.)

Who are the important characters in this story? (Call on different children. Ideas: *Atalanta, King Iasus, Ciron, Melanion, Aphrodite.* Record on chart.)

Tell me a word that describes each character. (Call on different children. Accept two words for each character. Record on chart.)

Where does this story take place? (Call on a child. Ideas: *In a kingdom, in a palace, on a mountain, in a field by the sea.* Record on chart.)

When does this story take place? (Call on a child. Ideas: *Long ago, in the past.* Record on chart.)

What was Atalanta's first problem in the story? (Call on a child. Idea: *Her father sent her out to die.* Record on chart.)

How did that problem make Atalanta feel? (Call on a child. Idea: *She wouldn't know because she was just a little baby.*) We don't know how she felt, so we will leave this box blank.

What attempts were made to help Atalanta solve her problem? (Call on a child. Idea: *The bear saved her.* Record on chart.)

What was the solution to Atalanta's problem? (Call on a child. Idea: *The hunter saved her.* Record on chart.)

Technology

(Children can research Greek myths, gods, and the Olympics on the Internet or in a children's version of an electronic encyclopedia.)

ADDITIONAL LITERATURE

Following are some additional titles that your students may enjoy during and following this lesson.

The Gods and Goddesses of Olympus by Aliki

Perseus by Warwick Hutton

Cyclops by Leonard Everett Fisher

Lesson 10

Language Skills Development

Skills: Proofreading for correct use of quotation marks
Time Required: 15 minutes

When characters in a story talk out loud, it is called dialogue. What is it called when the characters in a story talk out loud? (Signal.) *Dialogue.* When authors write stories they use punctuation marks called quotation marks to show that someone is talking. What do we call the punctuation marks that authors use to show that someone is talking? (Signal.) *Quotation marks.*

(Write sentence on the chalkboard. **The king asked, What do you want me to do?** Touch under each word of the sentence as the children read aloud.) Read the sentence. (Signal.) *The king asked, What do you want me to do?* What did the king ask? (Signal.) *What do you want me to do?*

Quotation marks that are put before what the character says look like sixes. (Draw a set of opening quotation marks before the word **what.**) Quotation marks that are put at the end of what the character says look like nines. (Draw a set of closing quotation marks on the chalkboard after the **question mark.**)

(Write sentence on the chalkboard. **The teacher says, I want all of you to put your work away.** Touch under each word of the sentence as the children read aloud.) Read the sentence. (Signal.) *The teacher says, I want all of you to put your work away.* What did the teacher say? (Signal.) *I want all of you to put your work away.* Raise your hand if you can come up and put the first set of quotation marks in the correct place in this sentence. (Call on a child. *Child writes in quotation marks at the beginning of the quote. Marks should look like a pair of sixes filled in.*)

Raise your hand if you can come up and put the second set of quotation marks in the correct place in this sentence. (Call on a child. *Child writes in quotation marks after* **away.** *Marks should like a pair nines filled in.*)

(Repeat process for these sentences: **Mario called out, Let's go to the store. Hazel answered, Yes, I would like to go.**)

When you are writing stories and paragraphs of your own, remember to proofread your writing for the correct use of quotation marks.

Literature

> # *Raven:*
> # *A Trickster Tale from the Pacific Northwest*
> ## by Gerald McDermott

Prereading

Examining the Book

This is the book that I am going to share with you today. The title of this book is *Raven: A Trickster Tale*. What's the title of today's book? (Signal.) Raven: A Trickster Tale.

Gerald McDermott told this version of the story, so he is the author. Who is the author of this version of *Raven: A Trickster Tale*? (Signal.) *Gerald McDermott.*

Sometimes the same person writes the story and makes the pictures. Sometimes the author and illustrator are two different people. Gerald McDermott wrote this story and he made the pictures. Did the same person write the story and make the pictures for *Raven: A Trickster Tale*? (Signal.) *Yes.* Gerald McDermott is both the author and the illustrator of this book. Who is the author of *Raven: A Trickster Tale*? (Signal.) *Gerald McDermott.* Who is the illustrator of *Raven: A Trickster Tale*? (Signal.) *Gerald McDermott.*

Story Genre

There are many different kinds of stories. The story *Raven: A Trickster Tale* is a special kind of story called a legend. What kind of story is *Raven: A Trickster Tale*? (Signal.) *A legend.* A legend is a very old story. What's a legend? (Signal.) *A very old story.*

There are also different kinds of legends. *Raven: A Trickster Tale* is a special kind of legend called a **how things came to be** legend. What kind of legend is *Raven: A Trickster Tale*? *A how things came to be legend.* *Raven: A Trickster Tale* tells a story about how the sun came to be in the sky. What does *Raven: A Trickster Tale* tell the story of? (Signal.) *How the sun came to be in the sky.*

Reading the Story

I'm going to read the story aloud to you and show you the pictures. After I read the story to you, we will talk about the story. (Read the story with minimal interruptions.)

Discussing the Book

Story Pattern

Most books have a pattern. Let's see if we can figure out the pattern for this book. You tell me what happened in the story and I'll write it on the chalkboard.

> **Note:** As the children retell the story, make a story map of the main story events on the chalkboard similar to the sample in Lesson 1.

(Discuss the sequence of story events briefly to construct the story map.)

(Point to the story map that is on the chalkboard.) Look at the shape of this story. It's a circle. This story starts and ends in the same place. What do we call a story that starts and ends in the same place? (Signal.) *A circle story.*

Characters and Setting

All stories have a beginning, a middle, and an ending. The beginning of a story tells about the characters that are in the story. What does the beginning of a story tell about? (Signal.) *The characters that are in the story.* Who are the most important characters in *Raven: A Trickster Tale*? (Call on different children. Ideas: *Raven, Sky Chief, Sky Chief's daughter.*)

The beginning also tells about the setting of the story. Raise your hand if you can tell us something about where the story *Raven: A Trickster Tale* happened. (Call on two or three children. Ideas: *The house of Sky Chief, Pacific Northwest, by the water.*)

Now let's think about when the story *Raven: A Trickster Tale* happened. (Flip through the first six pages of the book for the children to see.) What was different about the world at the beginning of the story? (Call on a child. Ideas: *It was dark. There was no sun.*) When do you think the world would have been all dark? (Signal.) *A long time ago.*

Story Problem

The beginning of a story often has a problem that changes the everyday life of at least one of the characters. What problem did Raven have in the story? (Call on a child. Ideas: *The world was dark. There was no sun.*)

In stories with a problem, the problem changes the feelings of the characters, so they decide to do something about the problem. How do you think Raven might have felt about his problem? (Signal.) *Sad.*

The middle of a story tells what the character does to try to solve a problem. This is called the attempt at solution. What did Raven decide to do about his problem? (Call on a child. Ideas: *Try to find the light. He tricked Sky Chief's family so that he could get the light.*)

The end of the story tells what happened that finally solved the problem. This is called the solution to the problem. What was the solution to Raven's problem? (Call on a child. Ideas: *He found the sun in a box. He stole the sun from the Sky Chief and put it in the sky.*)

Illustrations

(Point to the medal on the front cover.) This book is special because it won second prize for its pictures. This prize it won is called the Caldecott Medal. What prize did the book *Raven: A Trickster Tale* win? (Signal.) *The Caldecott Medal.* Raise your hand if you can tell us the name of another book we read that won this prize. (Call on a child. Ideas: A Chair for My Mother, Grandfather's Journey, John Henry.)

Let's look at the illustrations that Gerald McDermott made. There are many different ways to make illustrations for a book: you can paint them; you can draw them with a pen or pencil; you can make them with markers, crayons, or chalk. How do you think Gerald McDermott made his illustrations? (Call on a child. Ideas: *With watercolors, pencil crayons, pastels, and ink.*)

Recalling Information

Today we're going to finish our **Recalling Information** chart. Let's remember some of the things we learned about *Raven: A Trickster Tale,* and I'll write them down for you.

Note: Use the cumulative wall chart started in Lesson 1 for recording information from the "Recalling Information" activity in this literature lesson.

What is the title of today's book? (Signal.) Raven: A Trickster Tale. (Write the title on the chart.)

Who are the most important characters in this story? (Call on a child. Ideas: *Raven, Sky Chief, Sky Chief's daughter.* Record on chart.)

Tell me a word that describes these characters. (Call on different children. Accept two words for these characters. Record on chart.)

Where does this story take place? (Call on a child. Ideas: *In the world, the house of Sky Chief.* Record on chart.)

When does this story take place? (Call on a child. Idea: *A long time ago.* Record on chart.)

What was Raven's problem in the story? (Call on a child. Ideas: *The world was dark. There was no sun.* Record on chart.)

How did that problem make Raven feel? (Signal.) *Sad.* (Record on chart.)

How did Raven attempt to solve his problem? (Call on a child. Idea: *He tricked Sky Chief's family so that he could get the light.* Record on chart.)

What was the solution to Raven's problem? (Call on a child. Idea: *He stole the sun and put it in the sky for everyone to share.* Record on chart.)

Activity

Writing a Legend/Planning a Story/Drafting/Proofreading/Editing/Writing a Final Copy

Title: *How the Sun Came to Be in the Sky*
Materials Required: BLM 10, one copy for each child
Paper or notebook for writing story

Day 1

Procedure

1. (Show children a copy of *Raven: A Trickster Tale.*) This legend tells how the sun came to be in the sky. What does this legend tell? (Signal.) *How the sun came to be in the sky.*

2. You are going to write a legend about how the sun came to be in the sky. (Give each child a copy of the BLM 10.) First, you will make a plan for your story. Put your name on your planning sheet. (Check.)

3. Touch the first line on the planning sheet. You will write the title "How the Sun Came to Be in the Sky" on this line. (Check.)

4. Touch the next line. Write your name on this line. You are the author of this legend. (Check.)

5. Touch the next line. Read the word. (Signal.) *Problem.* What will the problem be for your stories? (Call on a child. Idea: *There is no light.*) Write the problem for your story on the line. (Check.)

6. Touch the word **Characters.** Touch the clusters beside the word **Characters.** Think about your story for a moment. (Pause.) Think about two characters that will be in your story. Write one character inside each circle. Then write words to describe what your character looks or acts like around each cluster. (Encourage children to use words that describe both appearance and personality.)

7. Touch the word **Setting.** Think about where and when your story happens. Write where and when your story happens.

8. Touch the word **Story.** What happens in a story is called the **plot.** What do we call the things that happen in a story? (Signal.) *The plot.* You will make a diagram to show the plot of your story. This story will begin and end in the same place. So, what will be the pattern for your story? (Signal.) *A circle story.* (Give children sufficient time to plan their stories.

Day 2

Procedure

1. (Have children write their own stories, following the story diagram they prepared on Day 1.)

2. (Give individual assistance as required to help children draft, edit, and proofread their stories. Encourage children to use proofreading marks to remind them where they need to make corrections.)

Day 3

Procedure

1. (Have children complete the final copy of their stories by hand or on a computer word processing program.)

2. (Have children make an illustration for their story using the designs and patterns used by the people of the Pacific Northwest as seen in *Raven: A Trickster Tale.*)

ADDITIONAL LITERATURE

Following are some additional titles that your students may enjoy during and following this lesson.

The Village of Round and Square Houses by Ann Grifalconi

Why Mosquitoes Buzz in People's Ears by Verna Aardema

Arrow to the Sun by Gerald McDermott

LEGEND PLANNING SHEET

Title _____

Author _____

Problem _____

Characters _____

Setting _____

Where _____

When _____

Story

Lesson 11

Language Skill Development

> **Parts of speech:** articles, nouns, verbs, adjectives, adverbs; writing simple sentences
> **Time Required:** 10–15 minutes
> **Preparation:** Write sentence patterns on the chalkboard: A+N+V, A+Adj+N+V, A+Adj+N+V+Adv.
> **Materials Required:** Class charts from Lesson 7, 8, and 9
> Paper and pencil for each pair of students

(Assign each child a partner.) Today you and your partner will see how many sentences you can make up for each sentence pattern that is on the chalkboard. You will take turns writing. Remember, you must make at least one sentence for each pattern. Ready? Go!

(Children should be expected to use capitals and periods correctly as taught in Lesson 5. Encourage children to write the sounds they hear in words and to use charts and dictionaries as sources for correct spelling. Children should be expected to correctly spell words taught in formal lessons.)

Literature

What Makes Day and Night

by Franklyn M. Branley

Illustrated by Arthur Dorros

Materials Required: Study lamp with focused light for experiment on pages 20–21.

Prereading

Examining the Book

This is the book that I am going to share with you today. The title of this book is *What Makes Day and Night.* What's the title of today's book? (Signal.) What Makes Day and Night.

The author of this story is Franklyn M. Branley. Who is the author of *What Makes Day and Night*? (Signal.) *Franklyn M. Branley.*

The illustrator of this book is Arthur Dorros. Who is the illustrator of *What Makes Day and Night*? (Signal.) *Arthur Dorros.*

Making Predictions

This book is a nonfiction book. It tells about true facts. What does a nonfiction book tell about? (Signal.) *True facts.* This book explains something that happens every day. What does this book explain? (Signal.) *Something that happens every day.*

(Assign each child a partner. Show children the front and back covers of the book.) Look at the front and back covers. Tell your partner what you think this book will explain. (Allow about one minute for sharing predictions.)

Raise your hand if you would like to tell us your prediction of what you think this book will explain. (Call on three different children. Accept reasonable responses.)

Reading the Story

I'm going to read the book aloud to you and show you the pictures. As I read the book we will stop and discuss things that the book explains.

Discussing the Book

(Read page 7.) Where do we all live? (Signal.) *On Earth.*

(Read page 8.) What shape is Earth? (Signal.) *Round.* Is Earth still? (Signal.) *No.* How does Earth move? (Signal.) *It spins.*

(Read page 10.) Why don't we feel it when Earth spins? (Call on a child. Idea: *Earth spins smoothly at the same speed.*)

(Read page 13.) How do we know that Earth is round? (Call on a child. Idea: *Spaceships have taken photos.*)

(Read page 14.) How long does it take Earth to spin around once? (Signal.) *Twenty-four hours.* What do we have as Earth spins through light, into darkness, and back again? (Signal.) *Day and night.*

(Read page 16. Point to the diagram of Earth.) The top of Earth is called the North Pole. What is the top of Earth called? (Signal.) *The North Pole.* The bottom of Earth is called the South Pole. What is the bottom of Earth called? (Signal.) *The South Pole.*

(Read pages 18 and 19. Review the diagrams with the children. Make sure that the children understand the rotation of Earth from sunrise to sunset.)

(Read pages 20–23. Conduct the experiment shown on pages 20–21. Discuss the experiment with the children. Ask them to tell you what each phase of the experiment represents. For example, phase one represents sunrise.)

(Read page 24.) How many miles does Earth turn each hour? (Signal.) *About one thousand.* What is Earth doing to you at sunrise? (Signal.) *Moving me toward the sun.*

(Read page 27.) What is Earth doing to you at sunset? (Signal.) *Moving me away from the sun.* (Point to the diagram.) Why does the sun seem to move across the sky? (Signal.) *Earth is turning.*

(Read page 29.) How long is each day and each night on the moon? (Signal.) *Two weeks.* How many times does Earth spin during one night on the moon? (Signal.) *Fourteen times.*

(Read page 30.) About how many hours of daylight do we have in twenty-four hours? (Signal.) *Twelve.* About how many hours of darkness do we have in twenty-four hours? (Signal.) *Twelve.*

Activity

Writing/Reading/Note-taking/Making a Plan/Labeling and Coloring a Diagram

Title: *Writing a Paragraph to Explain Why the Sun Comes Up*

Materials Required: One copy of the book *What Makes Day and Night*
one copy of the book *Raven: A Trickster Tale*
BLM 11, one copy for each child
Paper or notebook, pencil crayons, scissors, glue

Day 1

Procedure

1. (Show the children *Raven: A Trickster Tale.*) What did this story tell us about? (Call on a child? Idea: *How the sun got in the sky.*) Do you think it's true that we have a sun because a Raven pretended to be a baby, took it from Sky Chief's box, then put it in the sky? (Signal.) *No.* Stories that are about imaginary characters and events are called fiction. What do we call stories that are about imaginary characters and events? (Signal.) *Fiction.*

2. (Show the children *What Makes Day and Night.*) What things does the story *What Makes Day and Night* tell us about? (Call on two or three children. Ideas: *Why we have day and night; how Earth spins; what Earth looks like from space.*) Are the things that this story tells us about true? (Signal.) *Yes.* Stories that tell us about true facts are called nonfiction. What do we call stories that are about true facts? (Signal.) *Nonfiction.*

3. (Give each child a copy of BLM 11.) Today you are going to write a paragraph that explains why the sun comes up. You are going to write true facts about why the sun

comes up. Will your paragraph be fiction or nonfiction? (Signal.) *Nonfiction.*

4. You will make a plan before you write your paragraph. Touch the title on your planning sheet. (Check.) Read the title. (Signal.) *Planning Sheet for Writing an Explaining Paragraph.*

5. Touch the word that says **Question.** (Check.) You will start your paragraph with an opening sentence that asks a question. Raise your hand if you can ask a question about the sun coming up. (Call on a child. Idea: *What makes the sun come up?*) Write the question on the lines.

6. Touch the next set of lines. (Check.) Raise your hand if you can tell us a sentence that answers the question. (Call on a child. Idea: *Earth spins around once every twenty-four hours.*) Write the sentence on the lines.

7. Touch the box with people at A. (Check.) What time of the day are people at A having? (Signal.) *Sunrise.* Write **Sunrise** on the line under the box. (Repeat process for people at B, C, and D.)

8. Touch the lines that start with **People at A.** Write a sentence that tells what time of day people at A are having. (Give children time to write the sentence. Remind them about how sentences begin and end and to spell familiar words correctly. Repeat process for People at B, People at C, and People at D.)

9. Touch the words **Closing sentence.** (Check.) Paragraphs end with a closing sentence. How do paragraphs end? (Signal.) *With a closing sentence.* Raise your hand if you can tell us a sentence that you could use to end your paragraph. (Call on three or four different children. Idea: *This is why the sun comes up each day.*) Write the closing sentence that you would like to use at the end of your paragraph.

Day 2

Procedure

1. (Give children lined paper or notebooks.) Today you will write a paragraph to explain why the sun comes up. You will use the sentences from your planning sheet.

2. (Have children proofread their paragraphs and correct errors.)

Day 3

Procedure

1. (Ask children to write a good copy of their paragraphs on paper or in a notebook. The illustration from the planning sheet may be cut out, colored using colored pencils, and glued at the bottom of each child's paragraph. Display the illustrations on pages 18 and 19 from the book *What Makes Day and Night* for the children to refer to when coloring their diagrams.)

ADDITIONAL LITERATURE

Following are some additional titles that your students may enjoy during and following this lesson.

Musicians of the Sun by Gerald McDermott

Sun Up, Sun Down by Gail Gibbons

Planning Sheet for Writing an Explaining Paragraph

Question: _____

People at A _____

People at B _____

People at C _____

People at D _____

Closing Sentence: _____

Lesson 12

Language Skill Development

Writing complex sentences
Time Required: 30 minutes
Materials Required: Paper or notebooks.

Today you are going to write complex sentences. **Complex sentences** are hard sentences. What are complex sentences? (Signal.) *Hard sentences.*

One kind of complex sentence is a sentence that tells why. When you tell why, you use the word **because** in your sentence. What word do you use? (Signal.) *Because.*

My turn to write a complex sentence that tells why I like reading. (Write sentence on the chalkboard as you say it.) I like reading because I love stories. Read my sentence. (Signal.) *I like reading because I love stories.* Raise you hand if you can tell us a sentence that tells why you like reading. Remember to use the word **because.** (Call on different children. Accept responses that are a complex sentence using the **because** format.)

(Give each child a sheet of paper or notebook from previous lessons.) Write a sentence that tells why you like reading. (Check. Repeat process for **why I like recess, why food is good for you, why you don't run in front of cars.** Children should be expected to use capitals and periods correctly as taught in Lesson 5. Encourage children to write the sounds they hear in words and to use charts and dictionaries as sources for correct spelling. Children should be expected to correctly spell words taught in formal lessons.)

Literature

Rumpelstiltskin

By Paul O. Zelinsky

Preparation: Make two class charts: one titled "Words that Describe Evil Characters" and one titled "Words that Describe Good Characters."
Make a large cumulative chart. (See Recalling Information later in this lesson for a sample.)

Prereading

For a while we will be reading a special kind of stories called fairy tales. What kind of stories will we be reading? (Signal.) *Fairy tales.* The title of today's fairy tale is *Rumpelstiltskin.* What is the title of today's fairy tale? (Signal.) Rumpelstiltskin.

Rumpelstiltskin is a very old story that was first written down by two brothers, Jacob and Wilhelm Grimm, more than 150 years ago. The Grimm brothers lived in Germany, so they listened to German storytellers who knew the stories and then the Grimm brothers wrote them down in German. Who originally wrote the fairy tale Rumpelstiltskin? (Signal.) *Jacob and Wilhelm Grimm.* Paul Zelinsky retold the story in his own words, so he is known as the author of this version of the story. Who is the author of this version of the story? (Signal.) *Paul Zelinsky.*

Paul Zelinsky also made the illustrations for this version of *Rumpelstiltskin.* What do we call the person who makes the pictures for a book? (Signal.) *An illustrator.* Who illustrated *Rumpelstiltskin*? (Signal.) *Paul Zelinsky.*

Making Predictions

The cover of a book usually gives us some hints as to what the book is about. Let's look at the front cover for *Rumpelstiltskin* and make some predictions about the setting and the characters. Quietly choose a partner and make a prediction about the setting and the characters. (Allow one minute for sharing predictions.)

Sometimes the back cover of a book also has an illustration. Does the back cover of this book have an illustration? (Signal.) *Yes.* Does this illustration change any of the predictions you made when you looked at the front cover? (Call on a child. Accept reasonable responses.) Explain why. (Call on the same child. Accept a reasonable explanation.)

Reading the Story

I'm going to read this fairy tale aloud to you and show you the pictures. After I read the story to you, we will talk about the story. (Read the story with minimal interruptions—this ensures that the children hear the story in its entirety, thus helping them develop a better sense of story. Occasionally you may find it beneficial to discuss parts of the story that are complicated or have unfamiliar vocabulary.)

Discussing the Book

Before we read the story, we made some predictions about the setting and the characters. Think back and remember your predictions. Now we are going to verify those predictions. When you **verify** something, you check to see if it was true, or accurate. What do you do when you verify something? (Signal.) *You check to see if it was true, or accurate.* Verify your predictions with your partner. (Allow 30 seconds for verification.)

Who were the important characters in *Rumpelstiltskin*? (Call on different children. Ideas: *Rumpelstiltskin, the king, the miller, the baby.*) Let's describe Rumpelstiltskin. Do you think he was a good character or an evil character? (Call on different children. Idea: *Rumpelstiltskin was an evil character.*) What did Rumpelstiltskin do that showed he was evil? (Call on different children. Idea: *He made the miller's daughter promise to give him her first child.*)

(Point to the chart titled: "Words that Describe Evil Characters." Touch under each word as you read the title to the class.) The title on this chart says **Words that Describe Evil Characters.** What does the title say? (Signal.) *Words that describe evil characters.* We will keep a list of words that describe evil characters as we read different fairy tales. What are some words that describe Rumpelstiltskin? (Call on children. Accept correct responses and print them on the chart. You will add to this cumulative chart as you work through the different fairy tales.)

Now let's describe the miller's daughter. Do you think she was a good character or an evil character? (Signal.) *A good character.* What things did she do that showed she was a good character? (Call on different children. Ideas: *She obeyed her father. She kept her promise.*)

(Point to the chart titled: "Words that Describe Good Characters." Touch under each word as you read the title to the class.) The title on this chart says **Words that Describe Good Characters.** What does the title say? (Signal.) *Words that describe good characters.* We will keep a list of words that describe good characters as we read different fairy tales. What are some words that describe the miller's daughter? (Call on different children. Accept correct responses and print them on the chart. You will add to this cumulative chart as you work through the different fairy tales.)

The setting tells where and when the story takes place. Where did this story take place? (Call on a child. Idea: *At the king's castle.*)

Most fairy tales begin with a sentence that tells when the story took place. Sometimes that sentence begins with **Once upon a time.** What words do some fairy tales begin with? (Signal.) *Once upon a time. Rumpelstiltskin* begins with one word that means the same thing. *Rumpelstiltskin* begins with the word **once.** What word does *Rumpelstiltskin* begin with? (Signal.) *Once.* Does the word **once** tell exactly when the story took place? (Signal.) *No.* **Once** just tells that the story happened some time ago.

The beginning of this story presents a problem. What does the beginning of this story present? (Signal.) *A problem.* What was the problem in *Rumpelstiltskin*? (Call on different children. Idea: *The miller's daughter had to spin straw into gold and she didn't know how to do it.*)

The middle of the story tells what the miller's daughter did to try to solve her problem. What did the miller's daughter do to try to solve her problem? (Call on a child. Idea: *She took help from Rumpelstiltskin.*) How many times did Rumpelstiltskin help the miller's daughter? (Call on a child. Idea: *Three.*)

Rumpelstiltskin is an evil character, yet he helps the miller's daughter. Why does he do that? (Call on different children. Idea: *He wants more in return.*) What is the one thing Rumpelstiltskin really wants? (Call on a child. Idea: *He wants the miller's daughter's first child.*) Would a good character take a child from its mother? (Signal.) No.

Later, when Rumpelstiltskin came to get the baby, how many days did he give the queen to figure out his name? (Signal.) *Three.* How many guesses did she get each day? (Signal.) *Three.*

The ending of the story tells how the good character finally solved the problem and how she felt. How did the queen finally solve her problem? (Call on a child. Idea: *She guessed the name of the little man.*)

How do you think the queen felt at the end of the story? (Call on a child. Idea: *Happy.*)

What happened to Rumpelstiltskin? (Call on a child. Idea: *He flew out the window on his cooking spoon and was never heard from again.*)

Illustrations

Let's look at the illustrations Paul Zelinsky made. (Show two or three of the illustrations.) How do you think Paul Zelinsky made these illustrations? (Call on different children. Idea: *The illustrations are painted with oil paints.*)

(Show the first illustration of the queen and her child to the class.) How do you think the queen is feeling in this illustration? (Call on different children. Idea: *Frightened.*)

(Turn to the next page. Show the illustration to the class.) How do you think the queen is feeling in this illustration? (Call on different children. Ideas: *Frustrated, upset, she doesn't know what to do.*)

(Show children the page where the queen looks knowingly at Rumpelstiltskin and he shakes his fist in anger and frustration.) How do you think the queen is feeling in this illustration? (Call on different children. Ideas: *She looks unafraid. She looks like she knows what she is doing. She looks happier.*)

(Show children the last illustration of the queen and her child.) How does the queen look in this last illustration? (Call on different children. Ideas: *Happy, strong, unafraid.*)

Recalling Information

Let's remember some of the things we learned about *Rumpelstiltskin,* and I'll write them down for you.

> **Note:** Create a blank cumulative wall chart for recording information from the "Recalling Information" activity in this literature lesson. Draw it on large sheets of chart paper, because you will be adding to it during lessons 13, 14, and 15. See the following sample.

Title	Beginning	Ending	Good Character	Evil Character	Magic	Threes	Royal People and Places
Rumpelstiltskin							

What is the title of today's fairy tale? (Signal.) Rumpelstiltskin. (Record title on chart.)

How did the story begin? (Signal.) *Once.* (Record on chart.)

How did the story end? (Call on a child. Ideas: *Happily; Rumpelstiltskin was never heard from again.* Record on chart.)

Who was the good character in the story? (Signal.) *The miller's daughter.* (Record on chart.)

Who was the evil character in the story? (Signal.) *Rumpelstiltskin.* (Record on chart.)

Fairy tales usually have some kind of magic in them. Tell about the magic in *Rumpelstiltskin.* (Call on different children. Ideas: *Straw was spun into gold. Rumpelstiltskin had a flying spoon.* Record on chart.)

In fairy tales, things often happen in threes. Tell about the things that happened in threes in *Rumpelstiltskin.* (Call on different children. Ideas: *The miller's daughter spun three nights. She had three days to guess. She had three guesses each day.* Record on chart.)

Fairy tales often include royal people and places in the story. Tell about the royal people and places in *Rumpelstiltskin.* (Call on different children. Ideas: *King, queen, castle.* Record on chart.)

ADDITIONAL LITERATURE

Following are some additional titles that your students may enjoy during and following this lesson.

The Ugly Duckling by Hans Christian Andersen, adapted and illustrated by Jerry Pinkney

Goldilocks and the Three Bears retold by James Marshall

Hansel and Gretel retold by Rika Lesser

Lesson 13

Language Skill Development

Noun/Pronoun agreement
Time Required: 30 minutes
Preparation: Write the following sentences on the chalkboard:
1. Carla began to cry.
2. The man felt unhappy.
3. That book is the woman's.
4. This house is Mike's.
5. That car belongs to the boy.
6. These socks are the girl's.
Materials Required: BLMs 13A and 13B, one copy for each child; scissors; glue

Let's think about what you have learned about parts of speech. What do we call words used for persons, animals, places, or things? (Signal.) *Nouns.* What do we call the words **an, a,** and **the**? (Signal.) *Articles.* What do we call doing words? (Signal.) *Verbs.* What do we call describing words? (Signal.) *Adjectives.* What do we call words that tell how and when? (Signal.) *Adverbs.*

Today you are going to learn about another part of speech called pronouns. **Pronouns** are words that can take the place of nouns. What are pronouns? (Signal.) *Words that can take the place of nouns.* Here are some pronouns: **he, him, his, she, her, hers.** Raise your hand if you can tell us a pronoun. (Call on different children. *He, him, his, she, her, hers.* As children say each pronoun write it on the chalkboard in two columns without a heading. Put boy pronouns in one column and girl pronouns in the other column.)

Here is a rule about pronouns. Pronouns must agree with their nouns. Tell me the rule about pronouns. (Signal.) *Pronouns must agree with their nouns.* Boy pronouns go with boy nouns and girl pronouns go with girl nouns. Do boy pronouns go with girl nouns? (Signal.) *No.*

(Point to the pronouns listed on the chalkboard.) Look at how I wrote the pronouns on the chalkboard. Why do you think I put them in two columns? (Call on a child. Idea: *One column is for boy pronouns and one column is for girl pronouns.* Write headings above columns.)

(Point to the sentences that you wrote on the chalkboard.) Each of these sentences has a noun that can be replaced with one of these pronouns. (Point to the list on the chalkboard.)

(Point the sentence number 1.) Read the sentence. (Signal.) *Carla began to cry.* (Touch under the word **Carla.**) Is Carla a boy or a girl? (Signal.) *A girl.* So what kind of pronoun can we use for Carla? (Signal.) *A girl pronoun.* Raise your hand if you can tell us a girl pronoun that can replace the noun Carla. (Call on a child. *She.*) Say the sentence using the word **she** instead of **Carla.** (Signal.) *She began to cry.* (Repeat process for each sentence.)

We are going to play a game called Pronoun Bingo. (Give each child a copy of BLM 13A and BLM 13B.) The first sheet that I gave you is your Bingo card. The sentences for making your Bingo card and your Bingo pieces are on the second sheet that I gave you.

To get ready to play Pronoun Bingo you need to prepare your Bingo card. You will cut out the sentence squares and glue them in any square that you wish on your Bingo card. (Check. Give children sufficient time to cut out pieces.)

Next, cut out the game pieces at the bottom of your sheet and put them in a pile on your desk. (Check. Give children sufficient time to cut out pieces.)

Now you are ready to play. I will read aloud a sentence that is on your Bingo card. You will find the sentence. Then decide which pronoun could replace the noun that I say and cover that square. When you have four squares across, up and down, or diagonally, you may raise your hand and call out "Bingo!"

First item. The bus drove to the girl's house. What pronoun could replace **the girl's**? (Signal.) *Her.* That is correct. So place the word **her** over the sentence.

Second item. The boy got a kite kit. Cover the sentence with the pronoun that could replace the words **the boy.** (Repeat process for random items until a child has a Bingo.)

(This game should be played at least three more times to reinforce and practice noun/pronoun agreement. Bingo cards and pieces may be kept in small plastic bags with each child's name on the outside.)

Literature

Puss in Boots

By Charles Perrault

Illustrated by Fred Marcellino

Materials Required: Class charts titled: "Words that Describe Evil Characters" and
"Words that Describe Good Characters"
Recalling Information Chart started in Lesson 12

Prereading

Examining the Book

For a while we will be reading a special group of stories called fairy tales. What kind of stories will we be reading? (Signal.) *Fairy tales.* This is the next fairy tale that I am going to share with you. The title of today's fairy tale is *Puss in Boots.* What is the title of today's book? (Signal.) Puss in Boots.

Puss in Boots is a very old story that was first written down by Charles Perrault (per ROW) more than 300 years ago in France. Who is the author of *Puss in Boots*? (Signal.) *Charles Perrault.*

Fred Marcellino (mar chel LEE no) made the illustrations for *Puss in Boots.* What do we call the person who makes the pictures for a book? (Signal.) *An illustrator.* Who is the illustrator of *Puss in Boots*? (Signal.) *Fred Marcellino.*

Malcolm Arthur translated the story. A **translator** is the person who changes one language into another, like English into French. *Puss in Boots* was written in France, where the people speak French. Malcolm Arthur rewrote the story in English, so others could understand. What do we call the person who changes one language into another? (Signal.) *A translator.*

Making Predictions

The cover of a book usually gives us some hints as to what the book is about. Let's look at the front cover of *Puss in Boots* and make some predictions about the setting and the characters. Quietly choose a partner and make a prediction about the setting and the characters. **(Allow one minute for sharing predictions.)**

Sometimes the back cover of a book also has an illustration. Does the back cover of this book have an illustration? (Signal.) *Yes.* Sometimes both covers go together to make one picture. **(Open the book and show the children both covers at once.)** Do the front and back covers go together to make one illustration? (Signal.) *Yes.*

Reading the Story

I'm going to read this fairy tale aloud to you and show you the pictures. After I read the story to you, we will talk about the story. **(Read the story with minimal interruptions; this ensures that the children hear the story in its entirety, thus helping them develop a better sense of story. Occasionally you may find it beneficial to discuss parts of the story that are complicated or have unfamiliar vocabulary.)**

Discussing the Book

Before we read the story, we made some predictions about the setting and the characters. Think back and remember your predictions. Now we are going to verify those predictions. When you verify something, you check to see if it was true or accurate. What do you do when you verify something? (Signal.) *You check to see if it was true or accurate.* Verify your predictions with your partner. (Allow 30 seconds for verification.)

Who were the important characters in *Puss in Boots*? (Call on different children. Ideas: *Puss/the cat, the youngest brother, the king, the ogre.*) Let's describe the youngest brother. Was he a good character or an evil character? (Signal.) *Good.* What did he do that showed that he was a good character? (Call on different children. Accept reasonable responses. Ideas: *He helped Puss. He didn't kill the cat.*)

(Point to the chart titled "Words that Describe Good Characters.") We are going to add some new words that describe good characters to our class chart. Raise your hand if you can tell us some words that describe the youngest brother. (Call on different children. Ideas: *Handsome, youngest, poor.* Add new words to chart.)

Now let's describe Puss. Do you think he was a good character or an evil character? (Signal.) *A good character.* What things did he do that showed that he was a good character? (Call on different children. Idea: *He helped his master.*)

(Point to the chart titled "Words that Describe Good Characters.") Raise your hand if you can tell us some words that describe Puss. (Call on different children. Ideas: *Smart, good hunter.* Add responses to the chart.)

(Repeat this process for the remaining important characters.)

The setting tells us where and when the story takes place. Where does the story take place? (Call on one or two children. Accept reasonable responses. Ideas: *In a country where a king lived, in a place with castles.*) Most fairy tales begin with a sentence that tells when the story took place. Does *Puss in Boots* tell us exactly when the story took place? (Signal.) *No.* When does the story take place? (Call on a child. Ideas: *Long ago, before we were born.*)

The beginning part of this story presents a problem. What does the beginning of this story present? (Signal.) *A problem.* What was the problem in *Puss in Boots*? (Call on different children. Ideas: *The youngest brother had no money. He did not think he could live with only a cat.*)

The middle of the story tells what one of the characters did to try to solve the problem. Raise your hand if you can tell us what Puss did first. (Call on a child. Ideas: *He caught a rabbit for the king. He gave the king presents.*) Raise your hand if you can tell us what Puss did next. (Call on a child. Ideas: *He tricked the king and made him think that the youngest brother was the Marquis of Carabas. He made the king meet the youngest brother.*)

(Repeat this process until all the steps have been completed up to Puss eating the ogre.)

The ending of the story tells how the good character finally solved the problem and how everyone felt. What did Puss do when the ogre turned into a mouse? (Signal.) *He ate him.* Raise your hand if you can tell us how Puss solved the youngest brother's problem. (Call on different children. Ideas: *He made the youngest brother rich. He gave him a castle and the princess.*) How did the youngest brother feel at the end of the story? (Signal.) *Happy.*

Illustrations

Let's look at the illustrations that Fred Marcellino made. (Show two or three of the illustrations.) How do you think Fred Marcellino made these illustrations? (Call on different children. Accept reasonable responses. Idea: *The illustrations are painted with oil paints.*)

(Show the children the pictures with the ogre and Puss.) Who is bigger, the ogre or Puss? (Signal.) *The ogre.* (Show the children the picture with Puss leaping on the mouse.) But in the end, who is bigger? (Signal.) *Puss.*

Recalling Information

Let's remember some of the things we learned about *Puss in Boots,* and I'll write them down for you.

Note: Add the following information to the cumulative wall chart started in Lesson 12.

What is the title of today's fairy tale? (Signal.) Puss in Boots. (Record title on chart.)

How did the story begin? (Call on a child. Idea: *A miller had three sons.* Record on chart.)

How did the story end? (Call on a child. Idea: *Happily.* Record on chart.)

Who were the good characters in the story? (Call on different children. Ideas: *Puss, the younger brother, the king.* Record on chart.)

Who was the evil character in the story? (Signal.) *The ogre.* (Record on chart.)

Fairy tales usually have some kind of magic in them. Tell about the magic in *Puss in Boots.* (Call on different children. Ideas: *The ogre can change shapes. The cat can talk and walks on his back feet only.* Record on chart.)

In fairy tales, things often happen in threes. Tell about the things that happened in threes in *Puss in Boots.* (Call on different children. Ideas: *There were three brothers. The father left three things. Puss caught three animals. The ogre had three shapes.* Record on chart.)

Fairy tales often include royal people and places in the story. Tell about the royal people and places in *Puss in Boots.* (Call on different children. Ideas: *King, princess, palace.* Record on chart.)

 ADDITIONAL LITERATURE

Following are some additional titles that your students may enjoy during and following this lesson.

The Bremen-Town Musicians by the Brothers Grimm, retold and illustrated by Ilse Plume

Snow White and the Seven Dwarfs translated by Randall Jarrell, illustrated by Nancy Buckett

The Fisherman and His Wife translated by Randall Jarrell, illustrated by Margot Zemach

PRONOUN BINGO CARD

PRONOUN BINGO PIECES

Sandra found the missing cars.	That TV belongs to the man.	The book is in the woman's house.	The boy got a kite kit.
Aunt Ida handed me a dime.	Bill gave me a gift.	The bus drove to the girl's house.	That hat is Sarah's.
Give the mittens to Tim.	Those mops are Donna's.	The paper was on Dad's table.	That ice-cream cone is Father's.
Mom went back to the store.	This is Linda's map.	Sam liked to make things.	That dime is Don's.

he	he	he	him
him	his	his	his
she	she	she	her
her	her	hers	hers

Lesson 14

Language Skills Development

Skills: Proofreading for correct use of quotation marks
Time Required: 15 minutes

When characters in a story talk out loud, it is called dialogue. What is it called when the characters in a story talk out loud? (Signal.) *Dialogue.* When authors write stories they use punctuation marks called quotation marks to show that someone is talking. What do we call the punctuation marks that authors use to show that someone is talking? (Signal.) *Quotation marks.*

(Write sentence on the chalkboard. **His mother yelled, Watch out for cars!** Touch under each word of the sentence as the children read aloud.) Read the sentence. (Signal.) *His mother yelled, Watch out for cars!* What did his mother yell? (Signal.) *Watch out for cars!*

Quotation marks that are put before what the character says look like sixes. (Draw a set of opening quotation marks before the word **watch.**) Quotation marks that are put at the end of what the character says look like nines. (Draw a set of closing quotation marks on the chalkboard after the **exclamation mark.**)

(Write sentence on the chalkboard. **Ho, ho, ho, laughed the turtle.** Touch under each word of the sentence as the children read aloud.) Read the sentence. (Signal.) *Ho, ho, ho, laughed the turtle.* What did the turtle say? (Signal.) *Ho, ho, ho.* Raise your hand if you can come up and put the first set of quotation marks in the correct place in this sentence. (Call on a child. *Child writes in quotation marks at the beginning of the quote. Marks should look like a pair of sixes filled in.*) Raise your hand if you can come up and put the second set of quotation marks in the correct place in this sentence. (Call on a child. *Child writes in quotation marks after **ho.** Marks should look like a pair of nines filled in.*)

(Repeat process for these sentences: **I want to go with you, the little boy said. The cook shouted, Dinner is ready!**)

When you are writing your own fairy tale later in this lesson, remember to proofread your writing for the correct use of quotation marks.

Literature

Rapunzel

By Paul O. Zelinsky

Materials Required: Class charts titled: "Words that Describe Evil Characters" and "Words that Describe Good Characters"
Recalling Information Chart started in Lesson 12

Prereading

Remember that for a while we will be reading a special group of stories called fairy tales. What kind of stories will we be reading? (Signal.) *Fairy tales.* The title of today's fairy tale is *Rapunzel.* What is the title of today's fairy tale? (Signal.) Rapunzel.

Rapunzel is a very old story. Many different cultures have versions of the Rapunzel story. Paul O. Zelinsky used some ideas from the French, Italian, and German Rapunzel stories to make his own Rapunzel story. Paul O. Zelinsky retold the story in his own words, so he is known as the author of this version of the story. Who is the author of this version of the story? (Signal.) *Paul O. Zelinsky.*

Paul O. Zelinsky also made the illustrations for this version of *Rapunzel.* What do we call the person who makes the pictures for a book? (Signal.) *An illustrator.* Who is the illustrator of Rapunzel? (Signal.) *Paul O. Zelinsky.*

Making Predictions

The cover of a book usually gives us some hints as to what the book is about. Let's look at the front cover for *Rapunzel* and make some predictions about the setting and the characters. Quietly choose a partner and make a prediction about the setting and the characters. (Allow one minute for sharing predictions.)

Sometimes the back cover of a book also has an illustration. Does the back cover of this book have an illustration? (Signal.) *Yes.* (Point to the back cover.) What do you notice about this tower? (Call on a child. Idea: *It is the back of the tower that is on the front cover.*)

Reading the Story

(Read the book with minimal interruptions. Briefly explain any difficult words that children might not be expected to know. Ensure that children understand that **rapunzel** is an herb and that the girl, Rapunzel, was named after the herb.)

Discussing the Book

Before we read the story, we made some predictions about the setting and the characters. Think back and remember your predictions. Now we are going to verify those predictions. When you verify something, you check to see if it was true or accurate. What do you do when you verify something? (Signal.) *You check to see if it was true, or accurate.* Verify your predictions with your partner. (Allow 30 seconds for verification.)

Who were some of the important characters in *Rapunzel*? (Call on different children. Ideas: *Rapunzel, the sorceress, the prince.*) Let's describe the sorceress. Do you think she was a good character or an evil character? (Call on different children. Idea: *The sorceress was an evil character.*) What did the sorceress do that showed she was an evil character? (Call on different children. Accept reasonable responses. Ideas: *She made the woman give up her child. She sent Rapunzel and her babies away.*)

Would a good character make a mother give up her child? (Signal.) *No.* Why do you think the sorceress wanted Rapunzel? (Call on different children. Ideas: *She was lonely and wanted a child of her own. The father stole some rapunzel and the sorceress gave him some—the sorceress wanted to be paid.*)

(Point to the chart titled: "Words that Describe Evil Characters.") We are going to add some new words that describe evil characters to our class chart. What are some words that describe the sorceress? (Call on different children. Ideas: *Cruel, merciless, frightening.* Record responses on chart.)

Now let's describe Rapunzel. Do you think she was a good character or an evil character? (Signal.) *A good character.* What things did she do that showed she was a good character? (Call on different children. Ideas: *She was cheerful. She let her hair down when asked. She sang to the forest birds.*)

(Point to the chart titled: "Words that Describe Good Characters.") Let's add to our list of words that describe good characters. What are some words that describe Rapunzel? (Call on different children. Ideas: *Beautiful, sweet, beloved, dear.*)

The setting tells where and when the story takes place. Where did this story take place? (Call on different children. Ideas: *Three places: in Rapunzel's father's home, in the tower in the forest, and in the wild place.*)

Most fairy tales begin with a sentence that tells when the story took place. Sometimes that sentence begins with **Once upon a time.** What words do some fairy tales begin with? (Signal.) *Once upon a time. Rapunzel* begins with two words that mean the same thing. *Rapunzel* begins with the words **Long ago.** What words does *Rapunzel* begin with? (Signal.) *Long ago.* Do the words **long ago** tell exactly when the story took place? (Signal.) *No.* **Long ago** just tells that the story happened some time ago.

The beginning of this story presents a problem. What does the beginning of this story present? (Signal.) *A problem.* What was the problem in *Rapunzel*? (Call on different children. Ideas: *The sorceress locked Rapunzel in a tall tower in the forest. She couldn't get out.*)

The middle of the story tells what happened to Rapunzel that helped to solve her problem. What happened to Rapunzel that helped to solve her problem? (Call on a child. Ideas: *The prince came to visit her. The sorceress cut off her hair and sent her away to a wild place.*)

The ending of the story tells what finally happened that helped Rapunzel solve her problem. What happened so that Rapunzel and the prince could be happy together? (Call on different children. Ideas: *The prince found Rapunzel in the wild place. When the prince could see again, he was able to take Rapunzel and their children back to his home in the palace.*)

How do you think Rapunzel and the prince felt at the end of the story? (Call on a child. Idea: *Happy.*) What happened to the sorceress? (Call on a child. Ideas: *We don't know. The book doesn't say.*)

Illustrations

Let's look at the illustrations Paul O. Zelinsky made. (Show two or three of the illustrations.) How do you think Paul O. Zelinsky made these illustrations? (Call on different children. Idea: *The illustrations are painted with oil paints.*)

Sometimes illustrations tell us much of what the characters are feeling in the story. (Turn to the first illustration of the sorceress in the garden. Show it to the class.) How do you think the sorceress is feeling in this illustration? (Call on different children. Idea: *Angry.*)

(Turn to the page where Rapunzel is playing near a stream as a child. Show the illustration to the class.) How do you think the sorceress is feeling in this illustration? (Call on different children. Ideas: *Happy, like a mother might feel when she sees her child playing.*)

(Turn to the page where the sorceress is cutting off Rapunzel's hair.) How do you think the sorceress is feeling in this illustration? (Call on different children. Ideas: *Angry, hurt.*)

Recalling Information

Let's remember some of the things we learned about *Rapunzel,* and I'll write them down for you.

> **Note:** Add the following information to the cumulative wall chart started in Lesson 12.

What is the title of today's fairy tale? (Signal.) Rapunzel. (Record title on chart.)

How did the story begin? (Signal.) *Long ago.* (Record on chart.)

How did the story end? (Call on a child. Idea: *Happily.* Record on chart.)

Who were the good characters in the story? (Call on different children. Ideas: *Rapunzel, the prince.* Record on chart.)

Who was the evil character in the story? (Signal.) *The sorceress.* (Record on chart.)

Fairy tales usually have some kind of magic in them. Tell about the magic in *Rapunzel*. (Call on different children. Ideas: *Rapunzel had longer hair than any real person. Rapunzel's tears made the prince's blindness go away.* Record on chart.)

In fairy tales, things often happen in threes. Were there any threes in *Rapunzel*? (Signal.) *No.* (Record the word **none** on chart.)

Fairy tales often include royal people and places in the story. Tell about the royal people and places in *Rapunzel*. (Call on different children. Ideas: *The prince, the kingdom.* Record on chart.)

Activity

Day 1

Writing/Making a Plan/Listening

> **Title: *Planning and Illustrating a Fairy Tale***
>
> Materials Required: Summary wall chart from Lesson 12
> Class chart titled: "Words that Describe Evil Characters"
> Class chart titled: "Words that Describe Good Characters"
> BLM 14A, one copy for each child

Procedure

1. For the next five days, you will be writing and illustrating your own fairy tales. Before you write your own fairy tale, you need to make a plan. (Give each child a copy of BLM 14A.)

2. Raise your hand if you can tell us what the beginning of a fairy tale tells about. (Call on a child. Idea: *The characters in the story and the setting.*) Most fairy tales have at least one good character and one evil one. Think about the fairy tale you want to write. Think about a good character that you would like to use in your fairy tale. What does your good character look like? (Call on three or four different children. Accept appropriate responses.) What does your character do that shows he/she is a good character? (Call on three or four different children. Accept appropriate responses.)

3. Touch the first circle on Fairy Tale Planning Sheet Part 1. That circle is for your good character. Write the name of your good character in the circle. Next write some words that describe your character by the other lines coming out of the circle. (Point to the class chart titled: "Words that Describe Good Characters.") You may get ideas from the chart to help you describe your good character. (Give children 2 to 3 minutes to write. Circulate and encourage children to get their ideas down on paper. More than four ideas may be added to the cluster. Repeat process using other circle for evil character.)

4. What does the setting tell us? (Signal.) *Where and when the story takes place.* Think about your fairy tale. Write where your story will take place. Write when your story will take place.

5. Now think back to the fairy tales we have read. Raise your hand if you can tell us the name of one of those fairy tales. (Call on a child. Ideas: Puss in Boots, Rumplestiltskin, Rapunzel.)

6. Raise your hand if you can tell us what you notice about the titles of these fairy tales. (Call on a child. Idea: *They are the names of the characters.*) Some titles contain only the names of the good characters. Raise your hand if you can tell us the name of a fairy tale that has a good character's name as its title. (Call on different children. Ideas: Rapunzel, Puss in Boots.) Raise your hand if you can tell us the name of a fairy tale with an evil character's name as its title. (Call on a child. Idea: Rumpelstiltskin.)

7. Think of a name for your fairy tale. It might be the name of the good character, or the evil character, or even both. Write the name at the top of your planning sheet by the word **Title.**

8. Let's review the things that you have decided so far. You know the good characters, the evil characters, where the story takes place, when the story takes place, and the title. Tomorrow you'll finish planning your fairy tales.

Art

Title: *Illustrating the Covers of a Fairy Tale*

Time Required: 40 minutes

Materials Required: One copy of *Rumpelstiltskin, Puss in Boots,* and *Rapunzel*
Fairy Tale Planning Sheet Part 1, partially completed in writing lesson
Oil pastels
Manila tag covers, 8½ x 17 inches, marked in advance to indicate front and back covers

Procedure

1. Now that you have part of the writing planned, we will plan the illustrations. (Show children the covers of the fairy tales read in class.) Remember, some covers have two different pictures, and some have one joined to make one bigger picture. The covers usually give us information about the characters in the story and the setting.

2. (Hand out covers and pastels to each child.) Think about your characters. Look at your planning sheets and check what you wrote as descriptions of your characters. Find the part of your cover that will be the front, and use your pastels to draw a picture of your title character. Think about the colors you would use to show that someone is good or evil. After you have finished drawing the character, you could draw some things behind the character to show the setting. (Allow enough time for children to finish the front cover.)

3. Now think about the other characters. Read what you wrote on your planning sheet to describe the other characters. Find the part of your cover that will be the back, and use your pastels to draw a picture of the character that is not already on the front. Think about the colors you would use to show that someone is good or evil. Remember that you can draw both covers to be two different pictures, or you can make them parts of the same bigger picture. You can also draw behind the character to show the setting. (Allow enough time for children to finish the back cover.)

Note: When both front and back covers are finished, have children add the title and author's name, and if possible, laminate the covers for the children.

Day 2

Writing/Making a Plan/Listening

Title: *Planning and Writing a Fairy Tale*

Materials Required: Summary wall chart from Lesson 12
Class chart titled: "Words that Describe Evil Characters"
Class chart titled: "Words that Describe Good Characters"
BLM 14B, one copy for each child

Procedure

1. Today we will finish planning our fairy tales. Let's look back at the summary chart and remember how each of the fairy tales started. (Review the opening lines for the three fairy tales. Hand out BLM 14B.) Look at your second planning sheet. Write down the beginning words of your first sentence. The beginning of a fairy tale ends with a problem. Decide what problem your good character is going to have. Write the problem down on your planning sheet.

2. The middle of a story tells how one of the characters tries to solve that problem. Think about your good character and his or her problem. What is one thing he or she might do to solve the problem? Think of another thing he or she might do to solve that problem. Think of a third thing to solve the problem. Which of these ideas would work best? Save the best idea for last. Find the part of your planning sheet that shows **Middle** and write what your character will do first on line 1. Write the second thing the character will do on line 2. (Check.)

3. The end of the story tells how the good character finally solves the problem and how everyone feels. Find the part on your planning sheet that shows **Ending,** and write down your best idea for solving the problem. Write how the good character is feeling next to **Good Character,** and how the evil character is feeling next to **Evil Character.** Under this, write your very last sentence next to **Last Words.**

4. Most fairy tales also have magic, things that happen in threes, and royal people and places. Think about your story. Write down at least one magic thing that will happen; write down something that will happen in threes; and write down any royal people and places.

5. Let's review everything you have so far. You know the good and evil characters, where and when the story takes place, the title, the problem at the beginning, what the characters do in the middle, how the characters solve it at the end, magic, things in threes, and royal people and places. Next time, you'll write the beginning of your fairy tales.

> **Note:** The planning sheets should be collected and proofread before children begin the story.

Day 3

Writing/Listening/Art

> ## Title: *Writing the First Draft of a Fairy Tale* (Days 3–5)
>
> **Materials Required for Days 3–5:** Summary wall chart from Lesson 12
> Class chart titled: "Words that Describe Evil Characters"
> Class chart titled: "Words that Describe Good Characters"
> Completed Fairy Tale Planning Sheets (BLMs 14A and 14B)
> Lined paper or notebooks for rough drafts of stories
> Plain paper, markers, wax crayons, and colored pencils for illustrations

Procedure

1. Today you will write the beginning of your fairy tales. Let's look at your planning sheets and remember the stories you are going to write. You all have a good and an evil character, the title, and the setting. And on your second planning sheet, you have the beginning, the middle, and the ending. You have included magic, threes, and royal people and places.

2. Remember how your good character is going to show how he or she is good. Think also of how your evil character is going to show how he or she is evil. Read your words that you wrote to begin your story. Now it's time to start writing your story. When you have finished writing the part of your story that tells what the problem is, you will stop writing for today.

3. (Have children illustrate the beginning of their stories.)

Day 4

Procedure

1. Today you will write the middle of your fairy tales. Before you begin, read the beginning of your stories quietly to yourselves.

2. Let's look at your planning sheets again. Remember what you are going to write for your middle. Think about magic, threes, royal people and places. Today you will write about what your good character does to try to solve his or her problem. You will write about only the first two things he or she tries. What your character tries will not work or tell how he or she solves the problem. Will your character solve his or her problem in this part of the story? (Signal.) *No.* How he or she solves the problem will be for next time, at the ending. What part of the story will have the solution? (Signal.) *The ending.* Now it's time to write the middle. When you have finished writing what your good characters did to try to solve the problem, you will stop for today.

3. (Have children illustrate the middle of their stories.)

Day 5

Procedure

1. Today you will write the ending of your fairy tales. Before we begin, read the middle of your stories quietly to yourselves.

2. Let's look at your planning sheets again. Remember what you are going to write for your ending. Think about magic, threes, royal people and places. Today you will write about what your good character does to finally solve his or her problem and how everyone feels afterward. Now it's time to write the ending. When you have finished writing what your good characters did to finally solve the problem, you will stop, and your story will be finished.

3. (Assist children with editing and proofreading their completed stories. A final copy may be prepared by hand or word processed on the computer and assembled into a booklet or bound into a number of class books with three to four fairy tales in each book.)

4. (Have children illustrate the ending of their stories.)

Note: Once completed, the fairy tale books could be read to the class, with the illustrations shown. The collection could also be displayed in the library or placed in the classroom library.

ADDITIONAL LITERATURE

Following are some additional titles that your students may enjoy during and following this lesson.

Thorn Rose retold by Errol Le Cain

The Sleeping Beauty retold by Mercer Mayer

Hansel and Gretel retold by Rika Lesser

Name _____

FAIRY TALE PLANNING SHEET   PART 1

Title _____

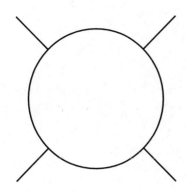

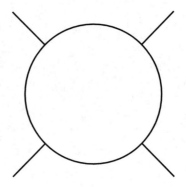

Setting

Where _____

When _____

Name _____

FAIRY TALE PLANNING SHEET   PART 2

beginning

first words _____

_____

problem   _____

_____

middle (trying to solve the problem)

1._____

_____

2._____

_____

ending (solving the problem)

_____

_____

feeling: good character _____

evil character _____

last words _____

magic	threes	royal people and places
_____	_____	_____
_____	_____	_____
_____	_____	_____
_____	_____	_____

Lesson 15

Language Skill Development

Subject/Verb Agreement
Time Required: 30 minutes
Preparation: Write the following sentences on the chalkboard:

They <u>was</u> going shopping.
Kim <u>were</u> making a kite.
The boys <u>is</u> eating ice cream.
That dog <u>are</u> howling.

Materials Required: BLM 15, one copy for each child; scissors

How we speak at school is called **formal language.** What do we call how we speak at school? (Signal.) *Formal language.*

(Point to the sentences on the chalkboard.) These sentences are not correct. They do not use formal language. (Touch under the first sentence.) This sentence says: **They was going shopping.** The correct way to say this sentence is: They were going shopping. Say the sentence correctly. (Signal.) *They were going shopping.* **Was** is not correct, so I cross out **was** and write **were** above it. Read the correct sentence. (Signal.) *They were going shopping.* (Repeat process for remaining sentences.)

Literature

Note: This will be a week-long lesson on dinosaurs. You will read three pages the first day, and four or five pages each day for the remainder of the week. As children learn about dinosaurs, collect and record information onto a class chart.

New Questions and Answers About Dinosaurs

by Seymour Simon

Illustrated by Jennifer Dewey

Preparation: Make a class chart titled "Things We Know About Dinosaurs" on large paper or chalkboard (not to be erased for the week). Use the following graphic organizer.

Materials Required: Six different colored markers

Day 1

This week you will be learning lots of information about dinosaurs. What will you be learning about this week? (Signal.) *Dinosaurs.* Later you will write your own report on a dinosaur.

Many of you already know lots of things about dinosaurs. Raise your hand if you would like to tell us something that you know about dinosaurs, and I will record it on this chart. (Point to the chart "Things We Know About Dinosaurs." Call on different children. Record responses on the chart. As children give an idea, record it as a cluster around the appropriate category. Allow children about three to five minutes for this activity.) What did you notice about where I wrote the information you gave me? (Call on a child. Ideas: *You wrote it around the categories or headings. You wrote things that describe dinosaurs around the word description.*)

Prereading

Examining the Book

This is the next book that I will share with you. The title of this book is *New Questions and Answers About Dinosaurs.* What's the title of today's book? (Signal.) New Questions and Answers About Dinosaurs.

This book was written by Seymour Simon. Who is the author of *New Questions and Answers About Dinosaurs*? (Signal.) *Seymour Simon.* The pictures in this book were made by Jennifer Dewey. Who is the illustrator of *New Questions and Answers About Dinosaurs*? (Signal.) *Jennifer Dewey.*

Today's book is an explaining book. The facts in this book are true, so this book is nonfiction. What kind of book is this? (Signal.) *Nonfiction.* Today's book is a collection of different kinds of information about dinosaurs. What is this book a collection of? (Signal.) *Different kinds of information about dinosaurs.*

Making Predictions

(Show children the front cover of the book.) The cover of a book usually gives us some hints on what the book is about. Let's look at the front cover of *New Questions and Answers About Dinosaurs* and make some predictions of what we think this book is about. (Give children a short time to share ideas with the class. Idea: *Dinosaurs.*) How many dinosaurs do you see on the front cover? (Signal.) *Five.* Are they all the same kind of dinosaur? (Signal.) *Yes.* What do you think the smaller ones are? (Call on a child. Idea: *Baby dinosaurs.*)

(Show children the back cover of the book.) What do you see on the back cover? (Call on different children. Ideas: *A flying dinosaur, a pteranodon or pterosaur.*) Do you think this dinosaur will be in the book? (Signal.) *Yes.*

Reading the Book

I'm going to read the first page of information about dinosaurs aloud to you and show you the picture. After I read the page to you, we will talk about it. The first page tells us the answer to this question: "What are dinosaurs?" What does the first page tell us? (Signal.) *The answer to the question: What are dinosaurs?* (Read the first page aloud.)

Discussing the Book

Raise your hand if you can tell us something new that you learned about what dinosaurs looked like from this page. (Call on different children. Ideas: *Dinosaurs are reptiles. They are big, small, two-legged, four-legged.* Record answers onto the class chart using a different color of ink.) Raise your hand if you can tell us something new you learned about what dinosaurs ate. (Call on different children. Ideas: *Meat, plants.*) Raise your hand if you can tell us something new that you learned about when dinosaurs lived. (Call on different children. Ideas: *The Mesozoic era, the Age of Reptiles, 65 million years ago.* Record answers on the class chart, adding a new category if necessary.)

(Show the children the table of contents at the beginning of the book.) Sometimes if a book has many different kinds of information to talk about, it has a table of contents at the beginning of the book. A **table of contents** tells the reader what information is in the book. What does a table of contents tell you? (Signal.) *What information is in the book.* The table of contents also tells you on what page you can find the information that you want to read about. What else does the table of contents tell you? (Signal.) *On what page you can find the information you want to read about.*

The next page of information I will read to you is "How Are Dinosaurs Different from Other Reptiles?" Raise your hand if you would like to come to the front of the class to tell us to what page I need to turn to find the second passage about dinosaurs. (Call a child to the front of the class and show him or her the table of contents.) *Page 7.* To what page do I need to turn to find the second passage on dinosaurs? (Signal.) *Page 7.* (Turn to page 7 and read the passage aloud.) Raise your hand if you can tell us something new that you learned about what dinosaurs looked like from this page. (Call on different children. Accept reasonable responses. Record answers onto the class chart.)

(Repeat process for page 8.)

Day 2

Today we will read more pages from *New Questions and Answers About Dinosaurs.* (Repeat process from Day 1 for reading pages 10–18. Be sure to ask children to come up to the front of the class to consult the table of contents before turning to the next passage on dinosaurs. Record new information that children learn each day with a different color marker to show cumulative learning.)

(Show children both pages of the index at the back of the book.) A list of the most important words and subjects in a book is called an **index.** What is a list of all the most important words and subjects in a book called? (Signal.) *An index.* An index lists all the important words and subjects in alphabetical order. How does an index list important words and subjects? (Signal.) *In alphabetical order.* An index also tells you on what page to find the important words and subjects. What else does an index tell you? (Signal.) *On what page to find the important words and subjects.*

Raise your hand if you would like to come up to the front of the class and tell us to what page we need to turn to find out about dinosaurs in Alaska. (Call on a child.) *Page 44.* Raise your hand if you would like to come up to the front of the class and tell us to what page we need to turn to find out about cold-blooded animals. (Call on a child.) *Page 36.* (Repeat process until every child has had a turn.)

Day 3

Today we will read more pages from *New Questions and Answers About Dinosaurs.* (Repeat process from Day 1 for reading pages 20–31. Be sure to ask children to come up to the front of the class to consult the table of contents before turning to the next passage on dinosaurs. Record new information that children learn each day with a different color marker to show cumulative learning. Repeat index activity with different topics.)

Day 4

Today we will read more pages from *New Questions and Answers About Dinosaurs.* (Repeat process from Day 1 for reading pages 32–41. Be sure to ask children to come to the front of the class to consult the table of contents before turning to the next passage on dinosaurs. Record new information that children learn each day with a different color marker to show cumulative learning. Repeat index activity with different topics.)

Day 5

Today we will read more pages from *New Questions and Answers About Dinosaurs.* (Repeat process from Day 1 for reading pages 42–45. Be sure to ask children to come to the front of the class to consult the table of contents before turning to the next passage on dinosaurs. Record new information that children learn each day with a different color marker to show cumulative learning.)

Activity

Question Writing/Making a Plan

Title: *Planning a Dinosaur Report*
Time Required: 20 minutes

Procedure

> **Note:** Display the class chart on dinosaurs to assist children in generating questions.

1. (Hand out a copy of BLM 15 to each child.) Later you are going to write a report about dinosaurs. People who do research on a topic first ask questions. What do people who do research do? (Signal.) *Ask questions.* Your topic for research will be dinosaurs. So, what will your questions be about? (Signal.) *Dinosaurs.*

2. Touch the box in the middle of your planning sheet. Read the word that is in the box. (Signal.) *Dinosaurs.* Touch the sentence at the top of the page that starts with the word **Questions.** Read the sentence. (Signal.) *Questions I have about dinosaurs.*

3. To get ready to do your research, you will write at least three questions about dinosaurs in the box. Make sure to start your question with a capital letter and end it with a question mark. You may look at the class chart for ideas and for the correct spelling of hard words. (Check.)

4. You will complete your research and the planning sheet later.

ADDITIONAL LITERATURE

Following are some additional titles that your students may enjoy during and following this lesson.

Dinosaurs by David Norman

Eyewitness Readers: Dinosaur Dinners by Lee Davis

Dinosaur Time (I Can Read Books Series: Level 1) by Peggy Parish

Things I didn't know about dinosaurs.

Questions I have about dinosaurs.

Dinosaurs

What could dinosaurs do if they came back?

imaginary

real

How big were the dinosaurs?

Lesson 16

Language Skill Development

Commas in a series

Preparation: Write the following sentences on the chalkboard:

That monster is huge and scary and ugly.

The boys found rocks and sticks and grass and feathers for making a nest.

Carl picked up hot dogs and buns and mustard and ketchup at the store.

Today you are going to learn about putting commas in sentences that have a list. (Write the following sentence on the chalkboard: **The crow found cheese and water and seeds.**) Read the sentence. (Signal.) *The crow found cheese and water and seeds.* (Touch the first **and.**) I can replace this **and** with a comma. Erase the word **and.** Put a comma after the word cheese. What can I use instead of the word **and?** (Signal.) *A comma.* Read the new sentence. (Signal.) *The crow found cheese, water and seeds.*

Here's a rule about commas. The last **and** in a list is not replaced by a comma. Is the last **and** in a list replaced by a comma? (Signal.) *No.* (Repeat process for the sentences that you wrote on the chalkboard.)

Literature

> **Note:** This book should be read over two days due to its length. As children learn more about dinosaurs, new information should be collected and recorded onto the class chart started in Lesson 15.

Dinosaurs Laid Eggs: And Other Amazing Facts about Prehistoric Reptiles

by Kate Petty

Illustrated by James Field, Mike Lacey, and Jo Moore

Prereading

Examining the Book

This is the next book that I will share with you. The title of this book is *I Didn't Know That Dinosaurs Laid Eggs.* What's the title of today's book? (Signal.) I Didn't Know That Dinosaurs Laid Eggs.

This book was written by Kate Petty. Who is the author of *I Didn't Know That Dinosaurs Laid Eggs*? (Signal.) *Kate Petty.* The pictures in this book were made by three different illustrators. How many illustrators made the pictures in this book? (Signal.) *Three.* James Field, Mike Lacey, and Jo Moore illustrated this book. Who are the three illustrators of *I Didn't Know That Dinosaurs Laid Eggs*? (Signal.) *James Field, Mike Lacey, and Jo Moore.*

Today's book is an explaining book. The facts in this book are true, so this book is nonfiction. What kind of book is this? (Signal.) *Nonfiction.* Today's book is a collection of different kinds of information about dinosaurs. What is this book a collection of? (Signal.) *Different kinds of information about dinosaurs.*

Making Predictions

(Show children the front cover of the book.) The cover of a book usually gives us some hints on what the book is about. Let's look at the front cover of *I Didn't Know That Dinosaurs Laid Eggs* and make some predictions about what we think this book is about. (Give children a short time to share ideas with the class. Idea: *Dinosaurs.*) How many dinosaurs do you see in the main picture on the front cover? (Signal.) *Three.* Are they all the same kind of dinosaur? (Signal.) *No.*

(Show children the back cover of the book.) Sometimes the back cover of a book gives us more information about what's inside. Do you see any of the same things on the back cover that you saw on the front cover? (Call on different children. Ideas: *A feather, the green dinosaur.*) (Read the back cover aloud.) What are some of the fun things you can do with this book? (Call on different children. Ideas: *Work on projects, seek out facts, take quizzes, find hidden objects.*)

Reading the Story

I'm going to read each page of information about dinosaurs aloud to you and show you the pictures. After I read the page to you, we will talk about it.

Discussing the Book

(Read page 5.) This first page is the introduction. The **introduction** tells us special information that the author wants us to know about the book. What does the introduction tell? (Signal.) *Special information that the author wants us to know about the book.*

(Point to the symbol that is in a pink box at the bottom of the page.) The author wants us to know that when you see this symbol that there is a fun project for us to try. What does this symbol mean? (Signal.) *That there is a fun project for us to try.*

(Point to the symbol that is in the blue box.) When we see this symbol, the author wants us to guess if the fact is true or false. I will ask you to guess if the fact is true or false before I read the information.

(Point to the exclamation mark.) This mark is an exclamation mark. What is this mark called? (Signal.) *An exclamation mark.* When you see this mark, the author wants us to check the borders for extra amazing facts. What will we do when we see this mark? (Signal.) *Check the borders for extra amazing facts.*

(Point to the exclamation mark symbol on page 6.) What does this mark mean? (Call on a child. Idea: *Check the border for extra amazing facts.* Read the fact aloud to the children. Repeat this process each time the children find the red exclamation symbol.)

(Point to the blue box symbol on page 7.) What does this symbol mean? (Call on a child. Idea: *Guess if the fact is true or false.* Read the fact aloud.) Raise your hand if you think this fact is true. Tell why you think this fact is true. (Call on a child. Accept reasonable responses.) Raise your hand if you think this fact is false. Tell why you think this fact is false. (Call on a child. Idea: *Humans were not on Earth at the same time as the dinosaurs.* Repeat this process each time the children find the blue box symbol.)

(Read pages 6 and 7.) Raise your hand if you can tell us something new on this page that you learned about when dinosaurs lived. (Call on different children. Accept correct responses. Record answers onto the class chart using a different color of ink.)

(Show the children the table of contents at the beginning of the book.) Sometimes if a book has many different kinds of information to talk about, it has a table of contents at the beginning of the book. A table of contents tells the reader what information is in the book. What does a table of contents tell you? (Signal.) *What information is in the book.* The table of contents also tells you on what page you can find the information that you want to read about. What else does the table of contents tell you? (Signal.) *On what page you can find the information you want to read about.*

The next page of information I will read to you tells us what the word **dinosaur** means. Raise your hand if you would like to come to the front of the class to tell us to what page I need to turn to find out what the word **dinosaur** means. (Call a child to the front of the class and show them the table of contents.) *Page 8.* (Read pages 8 and 9 aloud.) Raise your hand if you can tell us something new that you learned about dinosaurs. (Call on different children. Accept correct responses. Record answers onto the class chart using a different color of ink.)

(Repeat the reading procedure for each pair of pages from pages 10–17. Be sure to ask children to come up to the front of the class to consult the table of contents before turning to the next passage on dinosaurs.)

Activities

Reading/Listening/Speaking

Title: *Using a Glossary*
    Time Required: 10 minutes
    Materials Required: Copy of *I Didn't Know That Dinosaurs Laid Eggs*

Day 1

Procedure

1. (Show children the glossary at the back of the book.) This is a glossary. A glossary is a very short dictionary. What is a glossary? (Signal.) *A very short dictionary.* This book uses many difficult dinosaur names. The glossary tells us what these words mean. Why does this book have a glossary? (Call on a child. Idea: *To tell us what the difficult dinosaur names mean.*)

2. (Print the word **Ceratopsians** on the chalkboard.) This word says **Ceratopsians.** What word? (Signal.) *Ceratopsians.* (Print **dinosaurs with horns and a thick bone ruffle** on the chalkboard.) The glossary tells us what the word means. (Point to the meaning.) **Ceratopsians** means dinosaurs with horns and a thick bone ruffle. What does Ceratopsians mean? (Signal.) *Dinosaurs with horns and a thick bone ruffle.* (Repeat process for three or four more dinosaur names. This activity may be repeated more than once for further practice using a glossary. Other books about dinosaurs with a glossary may be placed in a center with job cards asking children to find the location of specific information.)

Day 2

Today we will read more pages from *I Didn't Know That Dinosaurs Laid Eggs.* What will we do today? (Signal.) *Read more pages from* I Didn't Know That Dinosaurs Laid Eggs.

(Repeat process from Day 1 for reading pages 18–29. Be sure to ask children to come up to the front of the class to consult the table of contents before turning to the next passage on dinosaurs. Record new information that children learn each day with a different color marker to show cumulative learning. Repeat glossary activity with different dinosaur names.)

Reading/Writing/Researching

> **Title: *Planning a Report***
> **Time Required:** 20 minutes
> **Materials Required:** Individual dinosaur report planning worksheets
> started in Lesson 15
> Cumulative class chart on dinosaurs started in
> Lesson 15

Procedure

1. Later you are going to write a report about dinosaurs. (Give each child his or her own planning sheet that was started in Lesson 15.) In the last lesson you wrote questions about dinosaurs. (Point to the class chart.) You have learned many new things about dinosaurs.

2. Touch the sentence at the top of the page that starts with the word **Things.** Read the sentence. (Signal.) *Things I didn't know about dinosaurs.*

3. To help you with your report, you will write at least three things you didn't know about dinosaurs, but you know now. You may look at the class chart for ideas and for the correct spelling of hard words. **(Check.)**

ADDITIONAL LITERATURE

Following are some additional titles that your students may enjoy during and following this lesson.

Dinosaur Babies by Lucille Penner

How Tough Was a Tyrannosaurus?: More Fascinating Facts About Dinosaurs by Paul C. Sereno

The Magic School Bus in the Time of the Dinosaurs by Joanna Cole

Lesson 17

Language Skill Development

Identifying base words and suffixes
Time Required: 20 minutes
Materials Required: One copy of the BLM dictionary from Lesson 2 for each child

Sometimes a word can have an ending added to it. Words that you can put endings on are called **base words.** What are the words we can put endings on called? (Signal.) *Base words.*

(Write the word **quick** on the chalkboard.) What is this word? (Signal.) *Quick.* (Write on the chalkboard: The quick fox ran past the gate.) Read this sentence. (Signal.) *The quick fox ran past the gate.*

Listen: I can add the ending **-ly** to the base word **quick** to make a different word. (Add **-ly** to the end of **quick.**) Now what does this say? (Signal.) *Quickly.* (Write on the chalkboard: **Mara ran quickly down the path.**) Read this sentence. (Signal.) *Mara ran quickly down the path.* What is the base word of quickly? (Signal.) *Quick.* What is the ending? (Signal.) *Ly.* What is the new word? (Signal.) *Quickly.*

(Write the word **miss** on the chalkboard.) What is this word? (Signal.) *Miss.* (Write on the chalkboard: **James is sad because he will miss his turn.**) Read this sentence. (Signal.) *James is sad because he will miss his turn.*

Listen: I can add the ending **-ing** to the base word **miss** to make a different word. (Add **-ing** to the end of **miss.**) Now what does this say? (Signal.) *Missing.* (Write on the chalkboard: **Dianna's gloves are missing.**) Read this sentence. (Signal.) *Dianna's gloves are missing.* What is the base word of **missing**? (Signal.) *Miss.* What is the ending? (Signal.) *Ing.* What is the new word? (Signal.) *Missing.*

(Give each child a copy of the BLM dictionary from Lesson 2.) Use your dictionaries to find some other base words with endings or to find base words to which you can add an ending. Raise your hand when you find a base word to which you can add an ending. (As children give a base word, write it on the chalkboard.) What endings can we add to this word? (Call on different children. Ideas: *Look, looking, looked, looks.*)

Literature

Note: As children learn more about dinosaurs, new information should be collected and recorded on the class chart started in Lesson 15.

How Big Were the Dinosaurs?

by Bernard Most

Prereading

Examining the Book

This is the next book that I will share with you. The title of this book is *How Big Were the Dinosaurs?* What's the title of today's book? (Signal.) How Big Were the Dinosaurs?

Sometimes the same person writes the book and makes the pictures. Sometimes the author and illustrator are two different people. Bernard Most wrote this book and he made the pictures. Did the same person write this book and make the pictures for *How Big Were the Dinosaurs?* (Signal.) *Yes.* Bernard Most is both the author and the illustrator of this book. Who is the author of *How Big Were the Dinosaurs?* (Signal.) *Bernard Most.* Who is the illustrator of *How Big Were the Dinosaurs?* (Signal.) *Bernard Most.*

Today's book is a nonfiction book. The facts in this book are true, so this book is nonfiction. What kind of book is this? (Signal.) *Nonfiction.*

Making Predictions

(Show children the front cover of the book.) The cover of a book usually gives us some hints as to what the book is about. Let's look at the front cover of *How Big Were the Dinosaurs?* and make some predictions of what we think this book is about. (Give children a short time to share ideas with the class. Idea: *Big dinosaurs.*)

(Show children the back cover of the book.) Sometimes the back cover of a book gives us more information about what's inside. Do you see any of the same things on the back cover that you saw on the front cover? (Call on different children. Ideas: *Children, a dinosaur.*)

Reading the Story

I'm going to read the story aloud to you and show you the pictures. After I read the story to you, we will talk about it. (Read the book aloud.)

Discussing the Book

(Read the first set of pages.) Raise your hand if you can tell us something new that you learned about the size of dinosaurs. (Call on different children. Idea: *Some dinosaurs were so big, three people could stand in one footprint.* Record answers onto the class chart using a different color of ink.)

(Read the next set of pages.) Raise your hand if you can tell us something new you learned about the size of dinosaurs. (Call on different children. Idea: *A Tyrannosaurus rex had teeth as long as a toothbrush.* Record answers on the class chart. Continue process for the remainder of the book.)

Illustrations

Let's look at the illustrations that Bernard Most made. There are many different ways to make illustrations for a book: you can paint them; you can draw them with a pen or pencil; you can make them with markers, crayons, or chalk. Bernard Most made his illustrations with a thick black pen and colored markers. How did Bernard Most make his illustrations? (Signal.) *With a thick black pen and colored markers.*

How do Bernard Most's illustrations make you feel? (Call on different children. Ideas: *Happy; they're funny.*) The pictures are funny and they look like cartoons. Does Bernard Most use bright, cheerful colors, or gloomy, dark colors to make his illustrations? (Signal.) *Bright, cheerful colors.*

Activities

Reading/Writing/Researching

> **Title: *Planning a Report***
>   **Time Required:** 20 minutes
>   **Materials Required:** Individual dinosaur report planning worksheets
>   started in Lesson 15
>   Cumulative class chart on dinosaurs started
>   in Lesson 15
>   Copy of *How Big Were the Dinosaurs?*

Procedure

1. Later you are going to write a report about dinosaurs. (Give each child his or her own planning sheet—BLM 15—that was started in Lesson 15.) In the last lesson, you wrote about the new things you have learned about dinosaurs. (Point to the class chart.)

2. Touch the sentence at the bottom of the page that starts with the word **how.** Read the sentence. (Signal.) *How big were the dinosaurs?*

3. (Show children the back inside cover of the book, which shows different dinosaur sizes.) The back of this book tells us that dinosaurs came in all different sizes. (Write on the chalkboard: **A stegosaurus is as big as a _____.**) When you say something is as big as or as small as something else, you're making a **comparison.** What's it called when you say something is as big as or as small as something else? (Signal.) *A comparison.* Raise your hand if you can think of something big we can compare a stegosaurus to. (Call on different children. Accept appropriate responses, keeping in mind that a stegosaurus was 30 feet long—as long as a city bus. To help children establish what a specific length is, you may wish to give the children yardsticks to measure how long the classroom is, or how long the hallway is. This will help them gain a better perspective of size for comparison. Encourage children to make a reasonable estimate; the exact answer is not necessary.)

4. To get ready to do your research, you will write in the box at least three comparisons for how big dinosaurs were. You may look at the class chart for ideas and for the correct spelling of hard words.

Activity

Reading/Writing/Making a graph as part of a report

> **Title: *Graphing the Size of Dinosaurs***
> **Time Required:** 20 minutes
> **Materials Required:** One copy of *How Big Were the Dinosaurs?*
> BLM 17, one copy for each child
> Colored pencils
> Various nonfiction books that tell about the size of dinosaurs

Procedure

1. Today we are going to make a bar graph to show the size of various dinosaurs. (Give each child a copy of BLM 17. Explain the process for coloring in a bar graph. Explain that each 10 feet of dinosaur length equals one square. The children will need to count by 10 as they color in the squares. Explain that 62 feet would be six squares plus a little bit of the next square to show two feet.)

2. Color your graphs neatly and carefully. You will be using this graph as one of the illustrations for your dinosaur report. (Check.)

3. (Have children record the names of at least three additional dinosaurs on the chart and graph their size. Encourage children to use various books to research for this additional information.)

ADDITIONAL LITERATURE

Following are some additional titles that your students may enjoy during and following this lesson.

The Littlest Dinosaurs by Bernard Most

Dinosaurs by Mary Pope Osborne and Will Osborne

Dinosaur Days (Step into Reading Books Series: A Step 2 Book) by Joyce Milton

The Size of Dinosaurs Graph

omeisaurus—66 feet												
shantungosaurus—52 feet												
supersaurus—80 feet												
parasaurolophus—33 feet												
hypselosaurus—40 feet												
Tyrannosaurus rex—50 feet												
triceratops—30 feet												
torvosaurus—33 feet												
ultrasaurus—100 feet												
stegosaurus—30 feet												
diplodocus—90 feet												
ankylosaurus—25 feet												
mamenchisaurus—72 feet												
apatosaurus—75 feet												
seismosaurus—120 feet												
allosaurus—35 feet												
brachiosaurus—85 feet												
baryonyx—30 feet												

Lesson 18

Language Skill Development

Dictionary Skills/Contractions, Compound Words, Synonyms, Antonyms
Time Required: 20 minutes
Materials Required: One copy of the BLM dictionary from Lesson 2
for each child

Today you are going to use your dictionaries to help you find different kinds of words.

Listen. A **contraction** is when two words are joined together and made shorter. What is a contraction? (Signal.) *When two words are joined together and made shorter.*

(Write on the chalkboard: **I am.**) Read these two words. (Signal.) *I am.* To make a contraction, I erase the **a** (demonstrate on the chalkboard) and write an apostrophe in its place (add an apostrophe). Next I rewrite the word without any spaces. (Write on the chalkboard: **I'm.**) Now this says **I'm.** What does this say? (Signal.) *I'm.* **I'm** is the contraction of **I am.** What is the contraction of **I am**? (Signal.) *I'm.* (Repeat process for **we are** and **could not.**)

Now it's your turn. Use your dictionaries to find some other contractions. When you find another contraction, raise your hand so that I can check if it is correct. What will you do when you find another contraction? (Signal.) *Raise my hand so you can check if it is correct.* (Give children two to three minutes to find contractions.)

Listen. A **compound word** is a long word made from two short words. What is a compound word? (Signal.) *A long word made from two short words.*

(Write on the chalkboard: **in.**) What word? (Signal.) *In.* (Write on the chalkboard: **side.**) What word? (Signal.) *Side.* Raise your hand if you can guess what compound word we can make with these two short words. (Call on a child. *Inside.*) To make these two short words into a compound word, I write them together without any spaces in between. (Write on the chalkboard: **inside.**) Raise your hand if you can tell me what this new compound word means. (Call on a child. Ideas: *The inner side or part; interior.* Repeat process for **doghouse** and **something.**)

Now it's your turn. Use your dictionaries to find some more compound words. When you find a compound word, raise your hand so that I can check if it is correct. What will you do when you find another compound word? (Signal.) *Raise my hand so you can check if it is correct.* (Give children two to three minutes to find compound words.)

Listen. A **synonym** is a word that means the same thing as another word. What is a synonym? (Signal.) *A word that means the same thing as another word.*

(Write on the chalkboard: **little, small.**) Read these words. (Signal.) *Little, small.* **Little** and **small** both mean the same thing, so they are synonyms. What are little and small? (Signal.) *Synonyms.* Raise your hand if you can think of another synonym for little and small. (Call on a child. Idea: *Tiny.* Repeat process for **bring/take** and **mend/fix.**)

Now it's your turn. Use your dictionaries to find some more synonyms. When you find a set of synonyms, raise your hand so that I can check if they are correct. What will you do when you find another set of synonyms? (Signal.) *Raise my hand so you can check if they are correct.* (Give children two to three minutes to find synonyms.)

Listen. An **antonym** is a word that means the opposite of another word. What is an antonym? (Signal.) *A word that means the opposite of another word.*

(Write on the chalkboard: **fast, slow.**) Read these words. (Signal.) *Fast, slow.* **Fast** and **slow** mean the exact opposite thing, so they are antonyms. What are fast and slow? (Signal.) *Antonyms.* (Repeat process for **lost/found** and **rich/poor.**)

Now it's your turn. Use your dictionaries to find other antonyms. When you find a set of antonyms, raise your hand so that I can check if they are correct. What will you do when you find another set of antonyms? (Signal.) *Raise my hand so you can check if they are correct.* (Give children two to three minutes to find antonyms.)

Literature

Day 1

If the Dinosaurs Came Back

by Bernard Most

Prereading

Examining the Book

This is the next book that I will share with you. The title of this book is *If the Dinosaurs Came Back.* What's the title of today's book? (Signal.) If the Dinosaurs Came Back.

Sometimes the same person writes the story and makes the pictures. Sometimes the author and illustrator are two different people. Bernard Most wrote this story and he made the pictures. Did the same person write the story and make the pictures for *If the Dinosaurs Came Back*? (Signal.) *Yes.* Bernard Most is both the author and the illustrator of this book. Who is the author of *If the Dinosaurs Came Back*? (Signal.) *Bernard Most.* Who is the illustrator of If the *Dinosaurs Came Back*? (Signal.) *Bernard Most.*

Today's book is a fiction book. The facts in this book are not true. They are make-believe. So, this book is fiction. What kind of book is this? (Signal.) *Fiction.*

Making Predictions

(Show children the front cover of the book.) The cover of a book usually gives us some hints as to what the book is about. Let's look at the front cover of *If the Dinosaurs Came Back* and make some predictions about what we think this book is about. (Give children a short time to share ideas with the class. Idea: *Very big dinosaurs.*)

(Show children the back cover of the book.) Sometimes the back cover of a book gives us more information about what's inside. Do you see any of the same things on the back cover that you saw on the front cover? (Call on different children. Ideas: *A city, cars, a dinosaur.*)

Reading the Story

I'm going to read the story aloud to you and show you the pictures. After I read the story to you, we will talk about it. (Read the book aloud.)

Discussing the Book

(Read the first two sets of pages.) Do you think that dinosaurs would really carry people to work and back? (Signal.) *No.* Real dinosaurs would probably stomp on the cars and eat the people, so carrying people to work is imaginary. Writing that can't really happen is called fiction. What is writing that can't really happen called? (Signal.) *Fiction.*

(Read the next set of pages.) Do you think in real life dinosaurs would make good lawn mowers or house painters? (Signal.) *No.* Real dinosaurs would probably stomp on the grass and damage the house. Writing that can't really happen is called fiction. What is writing that can't really happen called? (Signal.) *Fiction.*

(Repeat process for remainder of book.)

Illustrations

Let's look at the illustrations that Bernard Most made. There are many different ways to make illustrations for a book: you can paint them; you can draw them with a pen or pencil; you can make them with markers, crayons, or chalk. How do you think Bernard Most made his illustrations? (Signal.) *With a thick black pen and colored markers.*

What colors did he make the dinosaurs? (Call on different children. Idea: *Pink, brown, yellow.*) Do you think real dinosaurs were pink and yellow? (Signal.) *No.* Is anything else in the illustrations painted a color? (Signal.) *No.* Everything except the dinosaurs is drawn in black and white. How do Bernard Most's illustrations make you feel? (Call on different children. Ideas: *Happy, they're funny.*) The pictures are funny and they look like cartoons.

Activities

Skills: Reading/Writing/Researching

Title: *Planning a Report*

    Time Required: 20 minutes

    Materials Required: Individual dinosaur report planning worksheets started in Lesson 15

        Cumulative class chart on dinosaurs started in Lesson 15

        A selection of easy-to-read books on dinosaurs for children to use for research.

Procedure

1. Later you are going to write a report about dinosaurs. (Give each child his or her own planning sheet that was started in Lesson 15.) In the last lesson you wrote about the size of dinosaurs. (Point to the class chart.)

2. Touch the sentence at the bottom of the page that starts with the word **what.** Read the sentence. (Signal.) *What could dinosaurs do if they came back?*

3. First, think about some real, nonfiction things dinosaurs could do if they came back. For example, dinosaurs could live in a zoo. Raise your hand if you can think of another real, nonfiction thing that dinosaurs could do if they came back. (Call on different children. Accept responses that would be plausible in the real world.)

4. Next think about some imaginary, fictional things dinosaurs could do if they came back. For example, dinosaurs could wash all the windows in a skyscraper. Raise your hand if you can think of another imaginary, fictional thing that dinosaurs could do if they came back. (Call on different children. Accept all unreasonable and imaginary responses!)

5. To get ready to do your research, you will write in the box one real, nonfiction thing and one fictional, imaginary thing dinosaurs could do if they came back. You may look at the class chart for ideas and for the correct spelling of hard words.

Reading/Writing/Researching

Title: *Dinosaur Report*

    Materials Required: Individual dinosaur report planning worksheets started in Lesson 15

        BLM 18A, 18B, and 18C, one copy for each child

Note: Display the class chart on dinosaurs to assist children in brainstorming ideas about dinosaurs for their reports.

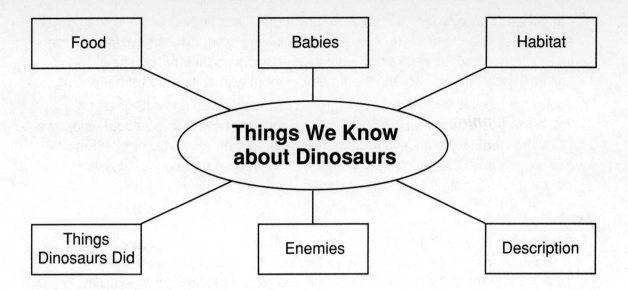

Things We Know about Dinosaurs

Food

Babies

Habitat

Things Dinosaurs Did

Enemies

Description

Day 1

Procedure

1. Today, you will begin writing a report about dinosaurs. (Pass out copies of BLM 18A to each child.) This is the first page of your dinosaur report. The first sentence in a paragraph is called the **opening sentence.** What is the first sentence in a paragraph called? (Signal.) *An opening sentence.*

2. The opening sentence has been written for you. Read the first sentence. (Signal.) *I had many questions about dinosaurs.* This is the opening sentence of the first paragraph of your report.

3. Read the part of the paragraph that has been written for you. (Signal.) *I had many questions about dinosaurs.* First I asked myself blank. Your job is to finish this sentence using the first question you wrote on your report planning sheet. What is your job? (Signal.) *To finish the sentence using the first question I wrote on my report planning sheet.* Write your questions on the lines. (Check. Repeat process for next two sentences.)

4. Touch the last sentence of the first paragraph. (Check.) Read the last sentence. (Signal.) *Now I will search for some answers.* The last sentence of a paragraph is called a **closing sentence.** What is the last sentence of a paragraph called? (Signal.) *The closing sentence.* If you have more than one paragraph in a report, the closing sentence can introduce the reader to the next paragraph. When the closing sentence introduces the reader to the next paragraph, it is called a **transition sentence.** What is a closing sentence called when it introduces the reader to the next paragraph? (Signal.) *A transition sentence.*

5. Now it's time for you to do some research. People who do research on a topic look for answers to questions. What do people who do research do? (Signal.) *Look for answers to questions.*

6. Touch the second paragraph of your dinosaur report. (Check.) Read the opening sentence aloud. (Signal.) *The next day I searched for the answers to my questions. I found out _____.* Now you will answer the three questions that you wrote. You will write your answers as sentences. These sentence answers will make the second

paragraph of your report. You may use any of the class books on dinosaurs as well as the class chart to help you research the answers to your questions. (Allow time for children to consult books and write their answers on their report sheets. As children write, circulate among them helping them with editing and proofreading.)

7. Touch the closing sentence. (**Check**.) Read the closing sentence. (**Signal**.) *Tomorrow you will learn about some more facts that I have learned about dinosaurs.* Does this closing sentence introduce the reader to the next paragraph? (**Signal**.) *Yes.* What do we call a closing sentence that introduces the reader to the next paragraph? (**Signal**.) *A transition sentence.*

Day 2

1. (Hand out a copy of BLM 18B to each child.) This is the second page of your Dinosaur Report. Touch the opening sentence. (**Check**.) Read the opening sentence. (**Signal**.) *The more I researched, the more I became intrigued with dinosaurs and wanted to learn more.*

2. For the third paragraph of your report, you will use the three things you learned about dinosaurs from your report planning sheet. Write three sentences to tell about what you learned about dinosaurs. These sentences will make the third paragraph of your report. (Encourage children to use the class books or class chart if they need ideas. As children write, circulate among them, helping them with editing and proofreading.)

3. Touch the closing sentence. (**Check**.) Read the closing sentence. (**Signal**.) *I was curious about the size of dinosaurs, so I pursued my research further.* Does this closing sentence introduce the reader to the next paragraph? (**Signal**.) *Yes.* What do we call a closing sentence that introduces the reader to the next paragraph? (**Signal**.) *A transition sentence.*

Day 3

1. (Hand out a copy of BLM 18C to each child.) This is the third page of your Dinosaur Report. Touch the opening sentence. (**Check**.) Read the opening sentence. (**Signal**.) *As I completed my research, I was amazed by what I found out about the sizes of dinosaurs.*

2. For the fourth paragraph of your report, you will use the three size comparisons you made about how big dinosaurs were from your report planning sheet. Write three comparison sentences on the lines. These sentences will make the fourth paragraph of your report. (Encourage children to use the class books or class chart if they need ideas. As children write, circulate among them, helping them with editing and proofreading.)

3. Touch the closing sentence. (**Check**.) Read the closing sentence. (**Signal**.) *My imagination began to soar.* Does this closing sentence introduce the reader to the next paragraph? (**Signal**.) *Yes.* What do we call a closing sentence that introduces the reader to the next paragraph? (**Signal**.) *A transition sentence.*

4. Touch the last paragraph of your Dinosaur Report. (**Check**.) Read the opening sentence. (**Signal**.) *Finally I thought about what would happen if the dinosaurs came back.* For your last paragraph, you will write one sentence that tells about a nonfiction or real thing about what dinosaurs could do if they came back. You will

write a second sentence that tells about a fiction or imaginary thing about what dinosaurs could do if they came back. (Encourage children to use the class books or class chart if they need ideas. As children write, circulate among them, helping them with editing and proofreading.)

Day 4

1. (Have children write or word-process a final copy of their reports. Ask children to choose any dinosaur they wish as an illustration for their reports. The illustration may be completed as a title page. Assemble reports, including the Size of Dinosaur graphs. Children may read their completed reports to classmates, children in other classes, or to parents or other adults. Reports may be displayed in the school or class library.)

ADDITIONAL LITERATURE

Following are some additional titles that your students may enjoy during and following this lesson.

A Boy Wants a Dinosaur by Hiawyn Oram

The Day of the Dinosaur by Stan and Jan Berenstain

Prehistoric Pinkerton by Steven Kellogg

Dinosaurs Report

I had many questions about dinosaurs. First I asked myself,

"_____

_____"

Next I thought about this question—_____

_____

Finally I thought _____

_____

Now I will search for some answers.

    The next day I searched for the answers to my questions. I found out _____

_____

_____

_____

_____

_____

Tomorrow you will learn about some more facts that I have learned about dinosaurs.

The more I researched, the more I became intrigued with
dinosaurs and wanted to learn more. _____

_____

_____

_____

_____

_____

_____

_____

I was curious about the sizes of dinosaurs, so I pursued my
research further.

As I completed my research, I was amazed by what I found out about the sizes of dinosaurs. _____

_____

_____

_____

_____

_____

_____

_____

My imagination began to soar.

Finally I thought about what would happen if the dinosaurs came back. _____

_____

_____

_____

_____

_____

Appendix

Title/Lesson	ISBN	Publisher
Lesson 1		
Dumpling Soup	0316730475	Little, Brown
Stone Soup	0874834988	August House
Mei Mei Loves the Morning	0807550396	Albert Whitman
Flyaway Girl	0316328669	Little, Brown
Lesson 2		
A Chair for My Mother	0688009158	Greenwillow
Tina's Diner	0689806345	Simon & Schuster
Cherries and Cherry Pits	083356630X	Econo-Clad Books
Music, Music for Everyone	0833513745	Econo-Clad Books
Lesson 3		
Dancing with the Indians	0823410234	Holiday House
Daisy and the Doll	0916718158	Vermont Folklife Center
Annie's Gifts	0940975319	Just Us Books
Rum-A-Tum-Tum	0823411435	Holiday House
Lesson 4		
Grandfather's Journey	0395570352	Houghton Mifflin
Song and Dance Man	0394993306	Alfred A. Knopf
The Lotus Seed	0152014837	Harcourt
Knots on a Counting Rope	0805054790	Henry Holt
Lesson 5		
Birdie's Lighthouse	0689835299	Simon & Schuster
My Nine Lives	0689811357	Simon & Schuster
Amelia's Notebook	0606183531	Demco Media
Castle Diary: The Journal of Tobias Burgess	0763604895	Candlewick
Lesson 6		
Dear Annie	0688135757	William Morrow
My Brother, Ant	014038345X	Viking Penguin
The Jolly Postman: Or Other People's Letters	0316126446	Little, Brown
Lesson 7		
Jeremiah Learns to Read	0531301907	Scholastic
The Wednesday Surprise	0395547768	Houghton Mifflin
Read for Me, Mama	1563973138	Boyds Mills

Title/Lesson	ISBN	Publisher
Lesson 8		
John Henry	0803716060	Penguin Putnam
Swamp Angel	0140559086	Viking Penguin
The Talking Eggs	0803706197	Penguin Putnam
Pecos Bill	0688099246	William Morrow
Lesson 9		
Atalanta's Race: A Greek Myth	0618051546	Houghton Mifflin
The Gods and Goddesses of Olympus	0064461890	HarperCollins
Perseus	0689505655	Simon & Schuster
Cyclops	0823410625	Holiday House
Lesson 10		
Raven: A Trickster Tale		
from the Pacific Northwest	0152656618	Harcourt
The Village of Round and Square Houses	0897197968	Weston Woods
Why Mosquitoes Buzz in People's Ears	0140549056	Penguin Putnam
Arrow to the Sun	0140502114	Penguin Putnam
Lesson 11		
What Makes Day and Night	0064450503	HarperCollins
Musicians of the Sun	0689807066	Simon & Schuster
Sun Up, Sun Down	015282782X	Harcourt
Lesson 12		
Rumpelstiltskin	0140558640	Viking Penguin
The Ugly Duckling	068815932X	William Morrow
Goldilocks and the Three Bears	0140563660	Penguin Putnam
Hansel and Gretel	0525461523	Penguin Putnam
Lesson 13		
Puss in Boots	0374361606	Farrar, Straus & Giroux
The Bremen-Town Musicians	0440414563	Bantam Doubleday Dell
Snow White and the Seven Dwarfs	0374468680	Farrar, Straus & Giroux
The Fisherman and His Wife	0374423261	Farrar, Straus & Giroux
Lesson 14		
Rapunzel	0525456074	NAL
Thorn Rose	014050222X	Penguin Putnam
The Sleeping Beauty	0027653404	Simon & Schuster
Hansel and Gretel	0525461523	Penguin Putnam
Lesson 15		
New Questions and Answers		
About Dinosaurs	0688081959	William Morrow
Dinosaurs	0881109886	EDC Publishing

Title/Lesson	ISBN	Publisher
Dinosaur Dinners	0789429594	DK Publishing
Dinosaur Time	0064440370	Harper Collins

Lesson 16

Dinosaurs Laid Eggs: And Other Amazing Facts about Prehistoric Reptiles	0761305963	Millbrook Press
Dinosaur Babies	0679812075	Random House
How Tough Was a Tyrannosaurus?	0448191164	Penguin Putnam
The Magic School Bus in the Time of the Dinosaurs	0590446894	Scholastic

Lesson 17

How Big Were the Dinosaurs?	0152008527	Harcourt
The Littlest Dinosaur	0152481265	Harcourt
Dinosaurs	0375802967	Random House
Dinosaur Days	0394870239	Random House

Lesson 18

If the Dinosaurs Came Back	0152380213	Harcourt
A Boy Wants a Dinosaur	0785722203	Econo-Clad Books
The Day of the Dinosaur	0394891309	Random House
Prehistoric Pinkerton	0606124861	Demco Media